CREATING YOUR ESTATE PLAN

18 RULES TO FOLLOW TO MAKE SURE YOUR ESTATE PLAN WILL WORK WHEN IT NEEDS TO

by Steve H. Hornstein, Esq.
Attorney at Law
CPA, LL.M., CFP®

Attorneys at Law
20335 Ventura Blvd., Suite 203
Woodland Hills, CA 91364
Office: (818) 887-9401 Toll-free: (888) 280-8100 Fax: (818) 887-7173
www.HornsteinLawOffices.com
www.HornsteinTrust.com

Copyright © 2019 by Steve H. Hornstein
ISBN: 978-0-578-22217-2

First Printing 2019
Printed in the U.S.A.
Library of Congress Cataloging-in-Publication Data
Creating Your Estate Plan by Steve H. Hornstein

First Edition

Cover and Book Design by
Shawn Kelly, kellygraphicdesign.com

DISCLAIMER

The purpose of this book is to educate and entertain. Neither the author nor publisher guarantee that anyone following the ideas, tips, suggestions, techniques, or strategies within it will become successful. The author and publisher shall have neither liability nor responsibility to anyone with respect to any loss or damage caused, or alleged to be caused, directly or indirectly, by the information contained in this book.

DEDICATION

To my family, my beautiful wife, Bryna,
and our children Ethan and Ella.
You are the purpose for all that I do.
Of course, without you, things would get done a little faster.

ABOUT THE AUTHOR

Steve Hornstein resides in Tarzana with his wife Bryna and their two children. The Hornsteins are active members of the Rotary Club of Woodland Hills, having hosted exchange students from France and Brazil. Steve is also active with the West Valley-Warner Center Chamber of Commerce, having served as its president and CFO and co-chair of the Chamber's Fine Wine and Food Tour that has grown to become a valuable event, helping its members connect with local businesses in the San Fernando Valley. Steve enjoys helping raise money for organizations vital to his community. In 2015, he danced the Tango at the Valley Cultural Center's "Dancing With Our Valley Stars" and took home a second place trophy! He also sang at a fundraiser for the Valley Women's Center. In 2019, he emceed the Miss San Fernando Valley and Miss Woodland Hills Competitions, official preliminary to the Miss America Pageant.

An avid runner, Steve enjoys running with his dogs Bailey and Riley, a 19 lb. poodle-bijan and an 11 lb. poodle. He achieved his running goals of a sub-4 hour marathon without his dogs, and a sub-20 minute 5k while running with his dogs!

Steve Hornstein has worked in the areas of accounting, tax, financial strategy, and estate planning since 1996, when he joined in the accounting firm of Deloitte & Touche, LLP in their Financial Counseling Services Group. At Deloitte, Steve worked in their offices throughout Southern California, on behalf of many business and individual high profile and high net worth clients. In 2000, Mr. Hornstein left Deloitte for a position as Controller of an internet consulting firm in Los

Angeles, CA, guiding the company through its sale to a venture capital firm in 2004.

Steve Hornstein opened Hornstein Law Offices and Hornstein Financial in Woodland Hills in 2002. His office assists clients not only in setting up their estate plans, but also in navigating through the entire estate and trust administration process when a loved one passes, including probate or other court petitions when necessary. Over the years, Hornstein Law Offices has prepared thousands of trusts and estate planning documents, and has successfully litigated nearly a dozen estate planning cases at trial. Hornstein Law Offices won the Daily News Readers Choice award for Best Living Trust for five years in a row! Steve is author of the comprehensive book on estate planning, "Creating Your Estate Plan – 18 Rules To Make Sure Your Estate Plan Will Work When It Needs To!"

Steve's current focus is to make quality estate planning efficient and affordable. Through his HornsteinTrust.com online trust preparation system he developed, people can create for themselves a low cost "Do It Yourself" estate plan or they can choose to meet with Steve or his staff for more comprehensive planning. "Too many people don't have a proper estate plan, and this creates turmoil for their families and unnecessary litigation in our already overcrowded courts. I see it every day. I want to help people protect their families, and in the process, help society as well."

Steve Hornstein's involvement with professional and civic organizations include the following:

• Member, California State Bar, 1996-present

• Certified Public Accountant, California, 1996-present

- Certified Financial Planner™ Certificant, 1999-present

- Series 7 and 63 licensed with HD Vest Financial - Series 7 since 1988

- California Department of Insurance, Life & Health license, 1995-present

- American Association of Attorney-CPAs (AAA-CPA), 1996

- American Institute of Certified Public Accountants (AICPA), 1996

- Financial Planning Association (FPA), 1999

- California Society of CPAs – Chairman San Fernando Valley CPA Discussion Group, 2003-4. Co-chair 2011-present

- Van Nuys Airport Citizens Advisory Council – Appointed by Councilman Dennis Zine, 2003-2006

- Woodland Hills Rotary – 2003-present; Secretary: 2006-2008

- Rose Goldwater Community Service Award, 2008

- West Valley ~ Warner Center Chamber of Commerce – President: 2005-2006 and 2014-2015 and 2015-2016; Treasurer: 2003, 2004, and 2005; Board member: 2007-present; CFO: 2009-2014 and 2016-present; Vice President: 2013-2014

- Financial Services Institute (FSI) 2017-present

- Northridge LeTip – President, 2019-present

TABLE OF CONTENTS

SO YOU'RE THINKING OF GETTING A TRUST OR SOME OTHER ESTATE PLAN

You have probably heard from friends or relatives, or seen on TV or read in the newspaper or on the internet, that it is important to have an updated estate plan. Perhaps you don't have an estate plan, or you have one that you signed before you had kids, or before you got married, and perhaps it hasn't been updated, or maybe you are wondering if the estate plan you got is set up correctly. If you do have an estate plan, you may question whether it does what you need it to do or what you intend for it to do. If you don't have an estate plan, you may be wondering if you need an estate plan at all, and if you do need some type of estate plan, what documents should you have prepared?

In Part 1 of this guide, I will begin with the basics and provide answers to these questions so that you can start taking action, if necessary, to protect yourself and your family.

In Part 2 of this guide, for those of you who find that some kind of estate plan is needed by you or a family member, I will present for you the "Hornstein Trust 18" – the eighteen rules of trusts and estate planning that should be followed or considered by anyone thinking of getting a Trust or other estate plan. In compiling my list, I considered problems I have seen arise in the past and how these problems could have been avoided. I also looked at what set of circumstances led families to easily sail through the estate planning seas with no problems, and how we can learn from how these people arranged their affairs. We can learn a lot by studying history, and this is what I am presenting to you. By no means is this list everything that should be considered. Certainly, there is more. But I believe this is a good starting point that will apply to most people who have or are considering getting Trusts or estate plans. Also, while there is almost no limit to how complicated an estate plan can be, I have not taken that bridge in this Guide to the more complicated estate planning techniques. When they come up, they can be discussed on a case by case basis. You may have heard of GRATs and GRUTs, and CRATs and CRUTs, and QPRTs and ILITs. These are all associated with estate planning techniques that are relevant to those with a larger "net worth," generally people with a net worth of over $10 million for a single person and $20 million for a married couple. If you have such a large estate, you should certainly be talking with your attorney, if not my office.

In Part 3 of this guide, I will explain the differences between having an estate plan prepared by an attorney with professional consultation, and a "Do-It-Yourself" estate plan. I will provide some of the issues to consider in helping you to choose which type of preparation is right for you.

Finally, in Part 4, I will explain how to get an appropriate and affordable Trust or other estate plan for you and your family with Hornstein Law Offices through the Hornstein Trust system.

This Guide is intended as a starting point. I feel comfortable in saying, "**Everyone who is, has, or is considering getting a Trust or other estate plan should start with this Guide.**"

Throughout this guide, I often use "him" and "her," or "he" and "she" interchangeably. Wherever possible, references are meant to be gender neutral.

Now, let's begin.

Caveat: This guide gets fairly detailed at times. If you are interested in knowing the details of estate planning, I encourage you to read this guide carefully, and then if you wish, you can move on to estate planning textbooks and even read the Probate Code. However, don't let your detailed reading cause you to delay in getting started with the preparation of your Trust or other estate plan. This guide is meant to help you, not cause you to procrastinate with your own important planning.

PART 1: THE BASICS

<u>What documents typically should be included in a complete estate plan?</u>

Typically, a complete estate plan should include the following documents:

1. Trust

2. Certification of Trust

3. Will(s)

4. Durable Power(s) of Attorney for Management of Property

5. Durable Power(s) of Attorney for Health Care (also called "Advance Health Care Directive(s)")

6. Physician's Directive(s)

7. Funding documents, to put your assets into, or "fund" your assets into, your Trust, because your Trust only governs what it owns! Such funding documents often include the following:

    a. Deed(s) to the Trust of real property such as your house

    b. Declaration(s) of Intent to evidence the intent to fund the Trust and to clarify separate and community property of spouses, as well as to clarify Trust and non-Trust assets

   c. Assignment of Property to fund the Trust with personal property (e.g. a car, jewelry, furniture, piano, clothes), or a business, or other property

   d. Specific Bequest Forms to provide instructions to the "Trustee" to give particular assets to particular beneficiaries. For example, you can provide that your guitar goes to your son but your piano goes to your daughter.

8. Instructions that are easy to read and understand, to explain how to get the documents executed (signed), and how to record the deed(s) with the county recorder. Instructions should also explain how to fund your Trust, and include an explanation of which assets you should fund into your Trust (transfer the ownership of the asset to the Trust) and which assets you should NOT fund into your Trust but instead change the beneficiaries.

9. Other documents as needed.

1) The Trust

There are several types of Trusts, but generally you may divide Trusts into two categories. Revocable Living Trusts and Irrevocable Trusts. Unless I specify otherwise, I am talking of the former, Revocable Living Trusts. As the name implies, a Revocable Trust is revocable by the creator, or "Settlor," of the

Trust. As the Settlor, you can change (or "amend") it, or you can revoke it altogether. A Revocable Living Trust is the type of Trust that is generally meant when people talk about getting a Trust to get their estate plan in order. **The most common reasons for getting a Revocable Living Trust is to get a plan to easily have your assets go where they are supposed to go after you pass away and avoid a costly "probate."** I will discuss the "probate" process in more detail later when I talk about what happens when someone doesn't have a Trust.

An Irrevocable Trust, on the other hand, as the name implies, cannot be changed. While this book won't extensively cover irrevocable trusts, one use of an Irrevocable Trust is to hold assets for the benefit of someone with a special need, or disability, that qualifies the person to receive benefits from the state or federal government, when the qualification to receive benefits would be lost if the individual had the funds outright. Such a Trust is called a Special Needs Trust. A Special Needs Trust can be used to supplement public benefits that a special needs child or adult may be receiving without disqualifying him or her from receiving public benefits.

Another type of irrevocable trust is an Irrevocable Life Insurance Trust ("ILIT"). An ILIT can reduce or eliminate "estate taxes" by having an Irrevocable Life Insurance Trust ("ILIT") own a life insurance policy so that the proceeds from the life insurance are outside the taxable estate of the insured person, so that the proceeds can go to the beneficiaries free of estate tax. Estate taxes don't apply to most people. You need to have a substantial net worth to be affected by estate taxes. That is, you must have a net worth that exceeds the estate tax exclusion amount, or have a large insurance policy that will cause your estate to be above the exempted amount. As of 2012, the estate tax exclusion amount was $5 million for a single person and double that, or $10 million for a married couple. The amount adjusts for inflation after 2012 such that it was $5,250,000 in 2013, $5,340,000 in 2014, $5,430,000 in 2015, $5,450,000 in 2016, and $5,490,000 in 2017. Under the Tax Cuts and Jobs Act, the biggest change to the estate tax in years, beginning January 1, 2018, the estate tax exemption rose from $5,490,000 to $11,180,000 per person ($22,360,000 for a married couple).* If your net estate, including life insurance, is approaching these levels, then an ILIT may be something for you to discuss with your estate planning attorney. I will discuss estate taxes in more detail later. If your estate is at the level where estate taxes may be an issue, then you should call your attorney and set up an appointment. Note that if your ILIT is the initial purchaser of your life insurance policy, then the proceeds of your life insurance will be outside of your estate immediately. However, if you are the purchaser, and then you transfer your insurance to your policy to your ILIT, you have to wait two years before the proceeds will be out of your taxable estate. The rules are complicated so it is important to discuss with an experienced estate planning attorney for help on how to best utilize an ILIT.

* The exemption is scheduled to increase annually with inflation, such that on January 1, 2019 the exemption rose to $11,400,000 ($22,800,000 for a married couple).

So, what exactly is a Trust? First, here is a complicated but accurate explanation of a Trust. A Trust is a "fiduciary relationship" with respect to property owned by the Trust, to which the "Trustee" holds legal title for the benefit of "beneficiaries," who hold equitable title. I know that is a mouthful, so I will simplify this. You may think of such a Trust as an "entity" that holds your property, as indeed, a Trust will typically hold your property. It will not cause you any harm to think of a Trust this way. But really, a Trust, a Revocable Living Trust, rather than being a separate entity, is simply an extension of yourself. It is another way to hold your property. You can hold it as an individual, or you can create a Trust to hold your property. So, while the Trust holds your property, it is not really held by a separate entity, but rather it is held by you as the owner and creator of the Trust (the "Settlor" or "Trustor") but with you as the Settlor assigning roles to the "Trustee" or "Trustees" (the person or people managing the property owned by the Trust) and the "Beneficiary" or "Beneficiaries" (the person or people for whose benefit the Trust property is held. And these roles are assigned to people within the Trust Agreement. The Trust is called an "Agreement" because the Trust is in essence an "Agreement"

> "When you put your assets into a Trust, roles of the owner, manager, and beneficiary are trifurcated into the three separate roles, all of which you may likely give to yourself, by making yourself the 'Trustor/Settlor,' the 'Trustee,' and also the lifetime "Beneficiary.'"

between the Settlor(s) and the Trustee(s) to set up the Trust and hold and manage and distribute property as provided in the Trust document.

To make this concept clearer, you are familiar with being the "Owner" of your assets, such as your bank account and investment account and house. You own them all. You are used to being the "Manager" of your property. You are the one with authority to write checks on your bank account. And finally, you are used to being the "Beneficiary" of your property. That is, all of your assets are for your benefit and enjoyment. This doesn't change when you put your assets into a Trust. When you put your assets into a Trust, the roles of the owner, manager, and beneficiary are trifurcated into the three separate roles, all of which you may likely give to yourself, by making yourself the "Trustor/Settlor," the "Trustee," and also the lifetime "Beneficiary."

The **Trustor,** also called the **Settlor,** is the creator of the Trust and also the ultimate <u>owner</u> of the assets, albeit through the Trust. When you set up a revocable Trust, the ultimate owner will always be you, or you and your spouse, if you set up a trust with your spouse. So in a revocable Trust, you can think of the Trustor as the owner of the assets, and that will always be you.

The **Trustee** is the <u>manager</u> of the assets owned by the Trust. Initially you will likely make yourself the Trustee, but you don't have to. Sometimes, perhaps later in life when someone is relying more on their son or daughter for assistance with their affairs, they may make their son or daughter a co-trustee or maybe even the sole trustee. Before we draft such a provision into the Trust document, we always review this issue carefully with the client to make sure it is appropriate. After you pass or if you become unable to act as Trustee, the successor Trustee that you designate will step up to the role of Trustee and follow the provisions in your Trust, which is your instruction book, as to how the Trust should be managed and how your assets should be distributed to the successor beneficiaries you choose.

The third party in a Trust is the **beneficiary**. During your life, you will likely make yourself the beneficiary, and you will name successor beneficiaries to receive your property after you pass. For example, you may provide that after you pass away, the Trustee will manage the Trust property for the benefit of your daughter until she is 30 years old and then the Trustee is to distribute the Trust assets outright to her. Or, if you and your spouse have a Trust together, you and your spouse can together provide in your joint Trust that the Trust property is to be held by the Trustee for the benefit of the surviving spouse until the surviving spouse passes away. Then after both spouses have passed, the Trustee is to hold the property for your daughter until she is 30 at which time

> **"In your Trust, you provide your instructions as to how you want your property to be managed and distributed after you pass away. You can make these instructions very specific to match the goals you have for your family."**

the Trust assets are to be distributed to her outright.

In your Trust, you provide your instructions as to how you want your property to be managed and distributed after you pass away. You can make these instructions very specific to match the goals you have for your family. Often, people leave their assets, or most of their assets, to their children. But again, this is your Trust and you can leave your assets however you wish. If you are married, I am generally talking about distributing after the passing of both spouses, as after the passing of one spouse, the assets may likely remain in Trust for the benefit of the surviving spouse. But, even here, you can choose something different. Some of our clients have chosen to have certain property distributed to a beneficiary other than a spouse upon one of the spouses passing. One client had a motorcycle he wanted distributed to their son upon his passing, and his wife had jewelry she wanted distributed to their daughter upon her passing. We can discuss if this may be applicable to you.

When you leave assets to a beneficiary through a Trust, you don't have to leave the assets outright. For example, you may not wish for your 12 year-old child to inherit property outright. Actually, a 12-year old would not be allowed by law to own property outright. It would have to be held by a guardian for them until they reach the age of majority. In California, the age of majority is 18; this is the age at which a person can enter into a contract. Still, most people would not want their 18-year old to inherit outright a large sum of money because such an inheritance may encourage poor choices in life, such as not buying a sensible car or not going to college if he or she would otherwise be a good candidate for college.

This is one of the great benefits of having a Trust. You can specify ages, or the occurrence of other conditions, at which you would like your children to inherit your assets. Until those conditions are reached such that the assets can be distributed outright to your children, the assets can stay in Trust and be managed by the successor Trustee of your Trust that you chose. Generally, you would allow your Trustee to make distributions as needed for your children's wellbeing, but your children won't receive their distributions outright until the conditions are met for outright distribution.

Many of our clients don't want their assets to go to their children until their children reach age 21 or 25. But you don't have to have your children merely reaching a certain age be the condition that must be met for them to receive their distribution outright. Through carefully drafted Trust provisions, parents can encourage their children to make smart choices. **If you and your spouse place a high importance on education, you could provide that your**

"If you and your spouse place a high importance on education, you could provide that your property will be distributed outright to your children at the age 25 if they have graduated from a four-year accredited university. Otherwise, they have to wait until age 30."

property will be distributed outright to your children at the age 25 if they have graduated from a four-year accredited university. Otherwise, they have to wait until age 30. This education condition is popular because parents often have high educational aspirations for their children, and they want to encourage their children to reach those aspirations. Age 25 may make sense because that is usually two to three years after they will have graduated from college, and they will have had two to three years to put their college degree to work for them before inheriting a sum of money. Also, by having to wait a few years after they graduate, instead of inheriting immediately upon graduation, they may be encouraged to not simply take easy courses to graduate in a hurry, but instead take courses that are meaningful to them and that they can use in a career. If you are not so particular that your child goes to a four year accredited university, you could simply require a "college degree" rather than a "degree from a four-year accredited university." The provisions you chose depend on your particular situation and what you desire for your children.

Through a Trust, you can choose a distribution that is appropriate to your family. For some of our clients, education is very important to their kids. For others, not as much. For those who aren't as demanding on their children as far as education, they may not require graduation from a four-year accredited university, allowing graduation of any college; a two-year degree would suffice. For someone who is a college professor, and desires that her daughter place the same high importance on education as the parent, the parent can provide that her daughter receives 1/3 of the Trust estate upon her daughter receiving a bachelor's degree, then half of the balance upon her attaining a master's degree, and finally, the balance upon her daughter attaining a Ph.D. I will discuss the math of this distribution later as problems can arise if provisions are not drafted properly to be mathematically correct.

Typically, if you are married, you and your spouse may likely have one Trust together. However, sometimes, in particular circumstances, a married couple will have one joint trust for their community property as well as one or two separate trusts for their separate property. This is not always necessary because a married couple's joint trust can hold both community as well as separate property of both spouses. Regardless, in certain circumstances, we may recommend separate trusts for your and your spouse's separate property. Attorney consultation is important to learn your particular circumstances, and identify issues in order to develop a plan that will protect you and your family.

Another very important benefit of a Revocable Living Trust is that when your assets are owned by your Trust, rather than you individually, your family and beneficiaries should not need to go through a probate. Probate is the court process of settling an estate, which I will discuss in more detail later.

2) Certification of Trust

A **Certification of Trust** will be important when you open accounts in the name of your Trust. The document tells the financial institution everything they need to know about your Trust in order to open an account in the name of the Trust, but leaves out private information that the financial institution does not need to know. For example, in order to open an account at a bank in the name of your Revocable Living Trust, the bank needs to know the name of the Trust, who is the Trustee, that the Trustee has the power to open a bank account, and the tax ID number of your Trust. As the Revocable Living Trust is an extension of yourself, the Tax ID number for your Trust will be your social security number. You will file your tax returns just as you always do. If you are married, then the spouse's social security may be used when you open a bank account in the name of your Revocable Living Trust. An Irrevocable Trust, by contrast, will have its own tax ID number separate from yours (or your spouse's if you are married). You will need to file a separate income tax return for an Irrevocable Trust.

3) The Will

As discussed more in Rule #8 of this guide, the Trust only governs assets owned by your Trust. You, as an individual, still manage assets that are owned by you as an individual. When you pass away, the successor Trustee of your Trust will have no power over assets you did not put into your Trust. Instead, assets you leave out of your Trust will be governed by your **Will**, which may have to go through a probate in court to administer. If you are married, you and your spouse will each have a separate Will even if you have one Trust together. A common goal of a proper estate plan is to fund assets into the Trust so that the value of assets governed by the Will are little to none. This way, a probate can be avoided. Probate is discussed further in Part 1 of this guide.

If you have minor children, your Will, or you and your spouse's Wills if you are married, will also provide who will be the "guardian" for your children until they reach age 18. While your pets are your property and thus may be "owned" by your Trust, your children are not your property. Rather, you are the "guardian" of your children. This is why the successor guardians for your children are covered in your Will instead of your Trust, which governs your property that you fund into your Trust. You could provide in your Will that your chosen successor guardian be the same person as the successor Trustee of your Trust, or you can separate their roles and have one person handle the money as successor Trustee of your Trust while another person or persons are guardians for your children. While the guardian will determine where the child or children live and go to school, the Trustee will handle the money and determine what gets paid. This is the way my wife and I drafted our Trust and Wills for our kids. It is not to say that that is always the right way to do it; it was just the right solution for our family. Keep in mind, there is no right and wrong way to do things; there is just the best way for your particular circumstances. Your attorney should discuss with you to find a solution that makes sense for you.

4) The Physician's Directive

The **Physician's Directive** is an important document in which you declare what life prolonging measures you wish to be made for yourself if you are in a persistent vegetative state or terminally ill, and life prolonging measures would only artificially delay death where the benefits do not exceed the costs. Most people generally do not wish to leave to someone else the responsibility of making decisions regarding whether to use life prolonging measures. Such a decision is often very difficult and emotional for someone to make on behalf of another person. You can make this decision for yourself in your Physician's Directive so that you do not have to burden anyone else with having to make this decision for you. In your Physician's Directive, you can make your instructions known to your doctor by making a declaration regarding your wishes, such as one of the following:

a) I do not wish to receive medical treatment if I am in an irreversible coma or persistent vegetative state; or terminally ill and life-sustaining procedures would only artificially delay death; or otherwise if burdens of treatment outweighs expected benefits.

b) I want to receive medical treatment that will allow me to live as long as possible.

If you have a spouse or domestic partner, each of you may make different choices. While I find that approximately 99% choose option (a), there is no right or wrong answer. The importance of making this decision for yourself made headlines with the legal battle involving Terri Schiavo in which Terri's husband and Terri's parents fought a very public battle in the Florida courts for seven years from 1998 until 2005 over the issue of whether to discontinue life prolonging measures. On February 25, 1990, Terri Shiavo suffered brain damage due to a lack of oxygen after collapsing in her home in full cardiac arrest. After two and a half months in a coma, her doctors changed her diagnosis to "vegetative state," and for the next two years her doctors tried therapy, without success, to increase her awareness. Finally, in 1998 Terri's husband filed a petition in court to have her feeding tube removed. Terri's parents opposed the petition. At one point her feeding tube was removed, only to be reinserted a few days later. Finally, after fourteen appeals and numerous other motions, petitions, and hearings, her feeding tube was finally removed for the last time on March 18, 2005, and she died thirteen days later. She had been in a coma for over fifteen years.

The case has been discussed and debated for years on issues including the sanctity of life, religion, and public policy. Both Terri Schiavo's husband and parents have written books on the case. While differing viewpoints remain among people, the legal battle started because of differing viewpoints of Terri Schiavo's husband and her parents. Determining which side was or is right or wrong from a public policy standpoint is not what a Physician's Directive seeks to answer. The purpose of the Physician's Directive is to inform your doctor what you think is right for YOU. "What would Terri Schavio have wanted for herself?" It was most unfortunate that Terri Schiavo's family never had a clear answer to this question because she never signed a physician's directive. It is a very important decision of whether to prolong your life by extraordinary measures when you are terminally ill or in a persistent vegetative state. Some may view it as cruel to leave the responsibility for making this decision on your behalf to someone else. Can you see yourself leaving to your children or parents this decision of whether or not to keep you alive? If you don't have a Physician's Directive, then you are leaving this decision to someone else. The Physician's Directive is the document in which you make the decision for yourself as to what you want for yourself as it pertains to using extraordinary measures to keep you alive when you are terminally ill or in a persistent vegetative state.

5) Durable Power of Attorney (Management of Property and Financial Affairs)

Durable Powers of Attorney ("DPAs") are especially important. I use the example that in the same way a Trust can avoid a "probate" of a Will (discussed later), a Durable Power of Attorney can avoid the need for a Conservatorship petition in court to appoint a Conservator to act on behalf of a Conservatee who has become unable to act for herself. There are two types of Durable Powers of Attorney. First, a DPA for Management of Property and Financial Affairs, and Second, a DPA for Health Care, also called an Advanced Health Care Directive. In a DPA for Management of Property and Financial Affairs, you, as the "Principal" (the creator of the DPA) appoint an "Agent" to handle your financial affairs if you become unable to handle your affairs. This is important not just for old people with a family history of Alzheimer's, but young people too. For example, I use the example that if I am in a car accident, who can handle my affairs and write checks on my account to pay my family's bills? My wife isn't on all of my bank accounts. The DPA will allow my wife to handle things until I am able, and if my wife is injured with me, then my Dad, and if my Dad can't or doesn't want to do it, then my brother can handle it. Remember the father who was horribly beaten at Dodger Stadium. I had heard on the radio that his family was having difficulty trying to get his affairs in order. His siblings were trying to find out how to get access to his bank accounts to pay bills. A Durable Power of Attorney would have allowed them to do this at a time when they already had too many difficult issues to manage.

It is important that the Power of Attorney (POA) be a "Durable" Power of Attorney (DPA), because a POA, called a "General Power of Attorney" if it is not durable, is only effective while the principal is able to act. Once the principal is not able to act, then the agent cannot act on behalf of the principal. However, with a DPA, the agent continues to be able to act on behalf of the principal even if the principal becomes unable to act, such as if the principal becomes incapacitated. Notwithstanding this, once the principal dies, the agent can no longer act on behalf of the principal.

As I will discuss in Part 2, in Rule #4, one shortcut some people do is simply add an adult child to their bank account so that if something happens to them, their adult child can access the account. This shortcut is often not a good idea because

CREATING YOUR ESTATE PLAN

there is little the parent can do if the child runs off with the money. When you add someone to your bank account, they are a co-owner with you! Not only may you be at risk of them taking the funds for their own personal purposes, but you may also be subjecting the bank account to the risk that your child's creditors may try to get at that account if, for example, your child has an auto accident with an expensive car and his insurance doesn't cover all of the loss! With a DPA, unlike with adding someone to your account, the funds do not belong to the agent you appoint, but rather your agent simply has authority to access the funds. Further, your agent has what's called a "Fiduciary Duty" to use the funds for your benefit, not your agent's benefit, and the funds won't be subject to the claims of your child's creditors!

I discuss powers of attorney in more detail in Rule #15 in Part 2.

6) Durable Power of Attorney for Health Care (Advance Health Care Directive)

In a **Durable Power of Attorney for Health Care,** also called an **Advance Health Care Directive**, you provide who can make health care decisions for you if you are incapacitated and can't tell the doctor yourself what you want done. If you don't have a DPA for Health Care, you may simply be leaving it up to the policy of the hospital and that may not be what you want. Further, you don't necessarily know what hospital you will be at. The policy of the hospital may be very different depending on which hospital you are at. For example, regarding decisions involving life support, a Catholic hospital may have quite a different policy than a Jewish hospital. When you have a DPA for Health Care, your agent can instruct the hospital the type of care to be provided and can have you moved to another hospital as <u>you</u> would have wanted.

Advanced Planning: My office generally has the DPAs effective immediately. Be careful if you currently have a DPA for financial affairs that allows your agent to act on your behalf only upon a doctor declaring you to lack capacity. The reason for this is that the Doctor won't be able to release information to the agent appointed in the financial DPA unless you also have a DPA for Health Care allowing the doctor to release the information to your agent. See Rule #15 in Part 2 for more on this issue.

7) Funding Documents

<u>Funding</u> is a critical part of setting up a Trust because the Trust only governs assets that it owns. The *funding* of a Trust is the process of putting your assets into your trust so that the assets are owned by your Trust. So how do you put assets into your Trust? If the asset is real estate, you put it into your Trust through a deed. When there is real estate, my office always prepares a deed and instructions for recording. We also provide an envelope to send the deed to the county recorder so that the real estate will be an asset of the Trust.

To fund financial assets such as bank accounts and investment accounts, we need to first examine what type of account we are talking about. Financial assets are generally divided into two categories which are treated differently in regards to funding your Trust. These categories are as follows: "Qualified" and "Non-qualified" assets. I term "qualified" assets as assets that are "qualified" under the Internal Revenue Code to receive tax-deferred or tax-free treatment, even if by the technically correct definition, insurance policies and annuities are not "qualified" account. For purposes of this discussion so that I don't overcomplicate things, I am including all retirement accounts and insurance policies and annuities under the umbrella of "qualified" accounts. Examples of such assets include retirement accounts such as IRAs and 401(k)s, and most insurance products such as life insurance policies that have a cash value and annuities. All other assets are "non-qualified." A bank account that is not a retirement account is a "non-qualified" asset. If you receive a Form 1099 reporting income you need to report on your tax return, then that account is a "non-qualified" account.

What to do with "Non-qualified" accounts: I recommend that you actually fund your non-qualified assets (e.g. non-retirement accounts) into your Trust. For example, you should go to the bank and have the account "titled" in the name of your Trust. Then the account is said to be "funded" into your Trust. To fund your non-qualified accounts such as a bank account into your Trust, you will take your Certification of Trust (in Section 1 of a Hornstein Trust book) to your bank and tell the banking representative that you set up a Living Trust and you want to fund the Trust with your bank account.

For other accounts such as your brokerage account, which, if an online account, may not have a branch office into which you can go, you can request a change of account form or speak with your financial representative regarding the forms needed to make the Trust the owner of your accounts. We offer to assist our clients as needed with transferring their assets to their Trust. Clients sometimes call my office from their bank so that we can walk them and their banker through the process. More and more, representatives at banks know what to do, but occasionally when a bank manager is not around, we can provide some helpful guidance to the banker to make things easier for you.

What to do with "Qualified" accounts: For "Qualified" accounts, you should call the financial institutions where you have accounts such as IRAs, insurance policies, and annuities, and request that they send you a "Change of Beneficiary Form." Retirement accounts, such as IRAs, 401(k)s, and the like, should NOT be titled into your Trust because changing the account owner may be treated as a withdrawal by the IRS such that your retirement account is taxable upon the change of ownership, even if the owner is simply changed to a trust of which you and your spouse are the owners and trustees. Therefore, you should change the beneficiary of such account.

If you are married, you can make your spouse the primary beneficiary and your Trust the contingent beneficiary. If the spouse is not the primary beneficiary of your retirement account, such as your 401(k) or IRA, your spouse will likely need to sign a "spousal consent" in order for your beneficiary designation to be valid. Insurance contracts, such as life insurance policies and annuities, are also "beneficiary driven." You should review and adjust the beneficiaries as needed.

While many estate planners commonly recommend that you name your spouse as the primary beneficiary and your Trust as the contingent beneficiary of qualified accounts including insurance policies and annuities, there is a good argument to naming your Trust as the primary beneficiary. Let's assume that you had your spouse as the primary beneficiary of your IRA and insurance policy and your Trust as the contingent beneficiary. Let's further assume that you passed away first and your spouse passed away two months later. If during that two months period, your spouse had not yet transferred the IRA to her own IRA, and also had not collected the proceeds of an insurance policy and put the proceeds into the Trust, the IRA and insurance policy account would be in your spouse's estate such that the IRA and insurance proceeds may have to go through a probate to get such assets into the Trust. Alternatively, if you had the Trust as the primary beneficiary rather than your spouse, the IRA and the insurance proceeds would go right to the Trust without any probate needed.

A Hornstein Trust book will include schedules of your non-qualified accounts to evidence your intention to fund these assets into your Trust. Your qualified accounts will be listed on a schedule of "non-Trust assets" showing your intent to not fund those accounts into your Trust.

As discussed, I recommend that you actually fund your non-qualified accounts (e.g. non-retirement accounts) into your Trust. However, when you try to fund your "non-qualified" bank account into your Trust, your banker may tell you that in order to fund your bank account into your Trust, the banker has to close your current account and open a new account in the name of your Trust. You may be thinking, "Oh, but that will be such a hassle because I have my automatic deposits and withdrawals set up for my account and it will be such a hassle to set this up all over again. For example, my social security or payroll checks get deposited automatically, and I am set up to pay my mortgage, cell phone, and cable bills automatically." If this is the case, perhaps speak with another banker to see if it is possible to keep your same account number but simply change the owner of the account to your Trust. If you are the only one on your current account and you are the only trustee of your Trust, your bank should be able to simply change the owner of your account to the Trust and keep your account number the same. The same result should apply if you and your spouse are the only signers on your old account and you and your spouse are the only trustees of your Trust. On the other hand, if you are the only one on your account but you and your spouse are the current co-trustees of your Trust, then the bank may not be able to simply change the account into your Trust, in which case, perhaps you can ask your banker to add your spouse to your account and then convert the account to be owned by your Trust. If ultimately, the bank says they can't do it and they need to open a new account and transfer your funds from your old account in your name to your new account in the name of your Trust, and that is not good for you, then there is another solution.

Your alternate solution is to simply **add a beneficiary to your bank account and make that beneficiary your Trust.** You do this by asking the bank for a POD ("Pay on Death") Form. For an account with a brokerage firm that holds securities such as stocks and bonds and mutual funds, the form is called a TOD ("Transfer on Death") Form. The logic is that you "pay" money in a bank account but you "transfer" securities in a brokerage account. On a POD or TOD form, you can provide that the primary beneficiary is your spouse (if you are married), and the contingent beneficiary is your Trust. If you are not married, then you may simply make your Trust your primary beneficiary.

I don't like adding a beneficiary to non-qualified accounts as much as actually funding the account into your Trust because it is more difficult to be certain that the beneficiary is actually added than it is to be certain that the account is funded into your Trust. If the Trust is merely a "beneficiary" of your account, your statements will not likely indicate this. Your bank statements often do not show that the POD beneficiary form is on file at the bank. Also sometimes, when one bank takes over another bank, which happened frequently around 2008, these POD forms may be lost. On the other hand, if you actually fund your account into your Trust, your bank statements will show your Trust as the owner so you will know it is funded into your Trust. If you use a POD or TOD form

STEVE H. HORNSTEIN, ESQ., CPA, LL.M., CFP®

rather than funding your account into your Trust, please be sure to get written confirmation from the bank that this has been done, and keep that written confirmation in an important place, such as with your Trust documents. Keep written confirmation from the financial institution for all accounts for which you name beneficiaries.

As I discuss in Part 2, I had a case where a financial advisor merely received telephonic confirmation that an insurance company had changed the beneficiary. When the time came for the beneficiary to collect on the policy, the insurance company denied receiving the change of beneficiary form.

If you have a business such as a closely held corporation or you are a member of a partnership, or you operate the business in another form such as a sole proprietorship or an LLC, a Hornstein Trust Book will include an **Assignment of Interest** to fund your interest in the business to your Trust. We also prepare a **general assignment** to assign your personal property into your Trust, along with a **Declaration of Intent** to show your "intention" to fund your Trust with your property.

How do you show how your **personal property** is to be distributed? While real property is real estate such as homes and apartment buildings and land, **personal property** includes many of the things inside the property, such as jewelry, art, musical instruments such as a piano and guitar, as well as vehicles. A complete Trust should contain **Special Bequest Forms**, which are forms to assist the Trustee in providing that specific property go to specific people. Such forms are always included in a Hornstein Trust Book. A client used to put post-it notes on all of their personal property with the name of the son or daughter or niece or nephew who should get that picture or lamp or piece of furniture after the client and her husband passed away. That seemed like a nice idea. But at holiday times, when the family came over for dinner, the kids and nephews and nieces would run around the house and switch the post-it notes. Then the kids who didn't get what they wanted would switch them back and check the next holiday to make sure that some other family member didn't switch the post-its again. Well, so much for the post-its idea for distributing personal property. That looked like a family feud in the making. I informed the client that a better solution for them might be to use the "Special Bequest Forms" that I would include in their Trust book. The forms are used to instruct the trustee as to whom to distribute personal property and are always found in the funding section of a Hornstein Trust Book. Property not listed on the Special Bequest Forms or mentioned elsewhere in the Trust is included in the remainder, and the Trustee will be able to distribute as part of the remainder or sell and distribute the proceeds from sale instead. The Trustee can also donate personal property to charity if doing so is better for the beneficiaries.

What if you don't have a Trust or you leave assets out of your Trust?

If someone does not have a Trust, then all of their assets are in their "estate" when they pass away. Remember that a Trust governs the assets that are in the Trust. A Will governs the assets that are in someone's estate. In California, if the gross value of the property in someone's estate is $150,000 or more, then the property must go through a court process called a **Probate** in order for the property to go to the beneficiary(ies) of the decedent's Will or the heirs of the decedent if the decedent does not have a Will. "Probate" is the court process to determine the validity of a Will and to give creditors an opportunity to file claims and ask the judge to pay them before the balance of the estate is paid to your beneficiaries of your Will, or heirs if you don't have a Will.

If the gross value of the property outside of Trust is less than $150,000, my office can prepare an Affidavit. A financial institution can accept an Affidavit in lieu of a court order, when the estate is less than $150,000. Along with the Affidavit, we also provide detailed instructions to the financial institution to transfer the assets to the Trust. If the estate is less than $150,000 but includes real property with a gross value of $50,000 or more, then a court order will still be required to transfer the real property.

The situation often arises in which someone passes away and property is found that is not in the Trust. Perhaps they bought property later, or they had an account that they did not fund into their Trust, or did not have a beneficiary on an account that needed a beneficiary, in which the default beneficiary would be the decedent's estate. Sometimes an individual refinances their house and the bank tells them that they have to take the property out of Trust to do the loan, perhaps because the banker doesn't want to take the risk that perhaps on page 58 of the Trust it says that the Trustee does not have the power to borrow money, which would NOT be an issue with a Hornstein Trust. But, with another Trust, to be safe, the financial institution may require that the borrower take the property out of Trust and do the refinance. Then the borrower can put the property back in Trust after the refinance is completed. However, all too often, the Borrower forgets to put the property back into the Trust after the refinance is completed. Then, when the owner passes away, the property is in the decedent's estate, not the Trust. Ordinarily, the property would have to go through a **probate** because it is in the decedent's estate.

Nevertheless, we may be able to fund into the Trust an asset inadvertently left out of Trust, and do it without a Probate. This can be done if we find certain documents that show the intention of the settlor to fund the asset into the Trust. One such document that shows the intent of the settlor to fund the Trust is a Declaration of Intent, which is typically included with a Hornstein Trust book. Another such document that shows intention to fund a Trust is an Assignment of Interest. If the Trust book is complete and contains the required documents, we may be able to file a special kind of petition in court called a "Heggstad petition" on behalf of the Trustee of the Trust (rather than on behalf of the Executor of the Estate as would be the case in a probate). Such petition will inform the court that it was the intent of the Settlors that such assets be transferred to the Trust but by forgetfulness or excusable neglect, the assets were not transferred. We then ask in the petition that the court order that such assets are in the Trust rather than in the Estate. We have been successful in many such petitions, and generally we can tell from a review of the documents if such a petition is appropriate and likely to succeed. To receive an order on a Heggstad petition takes much less time than a probate, possibly only three months, instead of the year, or more, that a probate takes, and is much less costly. But even better than waiting three months is waiting nothing by actually funding your Trust! See Rule #8 of this guide for more information on funding your Trust and how important it is to fund your Trust!

Years ago, I was in court for a hearing on a Heggstad petition that I had filed on behalf of the family of a decedent who had signed a Declaration of Intent with language prepared by another law firm. The decedent had inherited property after she had signed the Trust. I had filed a declaration of intent that had language that declared that she intended that all of her property was in Trust. It went on to say, "and henceforth, all of the decedent's property shall be held in Trust..." I attempted to argue that the "and henceforth" language meant that the property acquired through her inheritance "after" she signed the Declaration of Intent was meant to be held in Trust. The Judge responded, "Yes, I thought you were going to say that, but I think the 'and henceforth' language meant that everything she owned at the time she signed the Declaration of Intent would 'henceforth' be in Trust, not that property she acquired in the future would be in Trust." The Judge refused to order that the inheritance was in Trust. At the time, my office used similar language in our documents. However, ever since that day, we made sure that our Declarations of Intent specifically stated that <u>property acquired in the future</u> were also intended to be held in Trust. Of course, we were sure to omit tax qualified accounts such as IRAs (be sure to see Rule #8 for a discussion of what to fund and what <u>not</u> to fund into your Trust!).

A few years later, I had a case in which the decedent sold his house after he signed his estate plan and then purchased another house, but he forgot to deed his new house into his Trust. After he died, I filed a Heggstad petition requesting the Judge to order that his new house was in Trust so that we didn't have to go through a probate. Along with my petition, I attached his Declaration of Intent that included language to the effect that he intended any property acquired in the future should also be deemed to be in his Trust (excluding qualified assets discussed at Rule #8, of course). Based on my updated language in his Declaration of Intent, the Judge accepted our petition and ordered that his house was in Trust. I don't know if the family realized that the specific language my office has in our documents saved them over $15,000 in probate fees, but it did. Over the years, based on the experiences of my office either in court or in working with our clients in administering estates and

> "Over the years, based on the experiences of my office either in court or in working with our clients in administering estates and Trusts, we have made many adjustments to our documents that helped our clients avoid problems that they might have encountered had they not had a Hornstein Trust estate plan."

Trusts, we have made many adjustments to our documents that helped our clients avoid problems that they might have encountered had they not had a Hornstein Trust estate plan. They also saved money and time.

What about Estate Taxes?

I often hear middle class people complaining about the "death tax" and how wrong it is that the government will tax what they have left for their kids. To them I say that they may not need to worry about it. Estate tax only applies to the wealthy. For example, for a decedent who died in the year 2017, there will be no estate tax unless the net value of the estate is over $5,490,000, the Federal Estate and Gift Tax Exemption for the year 2017. If the decedent is married, then both spouses together can have double that amount before the estate tax applies. It is important to discuss with an estate tax attorney when a spouse passes because a IRS Form 706, *Federal Estate and Gift Tax Return*, may need to be filed in order to transfer the unused estate tax exemption to the surviving spouse.

If the net value of a decedent's estate is greater than the maximum Federal Estate and Gift Tax Exemption, then professional tax counsel should be hired in order to complete and file the Form 706 Estate Tax Return . This tax return reports the values of all assets which the decedent owned at the time of death, and then allows certain deductions, such as funeral expenses, debts, mortgages, and various other deductions to arrive at the "net taxable estate." Then a graduated tax is applied to that portion of the net taxable estate which is in excess of the Federal Estate and Gift Tax Exemption at a maximum 40% tax rate. The Form 706 Return must be completed within 9 months of the date of death. Assets must be valued exactly on the decedent's date of death or precisely 6 months after the date of death. Failure to file the 706 Return and the account for any tax which is due will result in severe penalties and interest on top of an already burdensome tax. The maximum Federal Estate and Gift Tax Exemption has changed over the years. Under the Tax Cuts and Jobs Act, the biggest change to the estate tax in years, the estate tax exemption rose from $5,490,000 to $11,180,000 per person ($22,360,000 for a married couple). You may have read that the exemption was rising to $11,200,000 in 2017. However, the CPI (Consumer Price index) that measures inflation was revised downward which reduced the estate tax exemption as well. The exemption is indexed to inflation, until 2025, at which time, the exemption goes back to the 2017 amount of $5,490,000 per person unless Congress changes the law. As I have never seen the exemption fall, except in 2011, when it went from infinity to $5,000,000, I do not expect the exemption to fall back to the 2017 amounts. But you can never be sure of anything, except for death and taxes, so it's best to be prepared for the unexpected. On the following page is a chart showing how the estate exemption has changed over the years.

FEDERAL ESTATE TAX EXEMPTIONS AND RATES OVER THE YEARS

Year	Estate Tax Exemption	Top Estate Tax Rate
1997	$600,000	55%
1998	$625,000	55%
1999	$650,000	55%
2000	$675,000	55%
2001	$675,000	55%
2002	$1,000,000	50%
2003	$1,000,000	49%
2004	$1,500,000	48%
2005	$1,500,000	47%
2006	$2,000,000	46%
2007	$2,000,000	45%
2008	$2,000,000	45%
2009	$3,500,000	45%
2010	$5,000,000 or $0	35% or 0%
2011	$5,000,000	35%
2012	$5,120,000	35%
2013	$5,250,000	40%
2014	$5,340,000	40%
2015	$5,430,000	40%
2016	$5,450,000	40%
2017	$5,490,000	40%
2018	$11,180,000	40%
2019	$11,400,000	40%

Without getting too technical, although this is difficult because this is a technical area, I should mention that under the American Taxpayer Relief Act of 2012 (ATRA), there is now a carryover of any unused exemption to a surviving spouse. In order to get that carryover, a Federal Estate Tax Return (Form 706) must be filed. There are types of trusts that provide that the Trust is split into two or more separate trusts upon the death of the first spouse; such trusts may be what is called an AB, ABC (QTIP) Trust, or a QDOT. For these types of trusts then upon the death of the first spouse, in addition to assessing the need to file the 706 Federal Estate Tax Return, a trust division statement will need to be prepared to transfer the correct amount of assets into each of the subtrusts created within the family Trust on the death of the first spouse. Likely, an attorney or CPA will do this work. In Part 2 of this guide, I discuss several kinds of Trusts that married people may choose, including a Marital Trust, an AB Trust, a Marital Disclaimer Trust, and an ABC Trust.

With the estate tax exemption amount rising to $11,180,000 in 2018, most people don't need to worry about estate taxes. Most people get an estate plan to avoid the costs of probate and to have an efficient plan in place to reduce costs and wasted time and potential family disputes. However, when one spouse is not a U.S. citizen, estate tax problems can arise for estates as low as $100,000. Drafting particular provisions into the Trust can help to reduce or eliminate these problems. It is often beneficial to consult an estate tax attorney regarding estate planning issues that you don't understand and to determine if any particular provisions should be incorporated into your documents.

Now let's look at rules to help make sure that your estate plan will work as you intend it to work!

PART 2: THE "HORNSTEIN TRUST 18"–
18 RULES TO AN ESTATE PLAN
THAT WILL WORK WHEN IT NEEDS TO

In this Part 2, I present my eighteen rules to an estate plan that will work. These eighteen rules must be followed or at least considered by everyone who either has or is considering getting a Trust or other estate plan. Otherwise, their families may become victims of the problems that commonly destroy plans that good intentioned people create for their families. In compiling my rules, I looked at the problems I have seen arise in the past and how they could have been avoided. I looked at what set of circumstances caused situations to easily sail through the estate planning seas with no problems, and how we can learn from how those estate plans were prepared. We can learn a lot by studying history. This is what I have examined in order to help you to have a plan that will work for you and your family. By no means is this list everything that should be considered. Certainly, there is more. This Guide is intended as a starting point. Without hesitation, I feel comfortable in saying that, **"Everyone who has, or is considering getting, a Trust or other estate plan should start with this Guide."**

Now, let's begin with **Hornstein Trust's 18 Rules to an Estate Plan That Will Work!**

Rule #1: Don't Procrastinate or You or Your Family May End Up In Court! Generally, everything is less expensive when done early. Specifically, estate planning works out best when you do it early.

I am going to ask you to do something now that will only take around 15 seconds and I promise that only good things can come of it, so there is no reason not to do this now. Take out your calendar whether you keep it on your phone, your iPad, on paper, or whatever you use to keep your schedule. Go to your calendar and go to the date exactly one month from today. On your schedule for that date one month from today, make an entry called, "Check Rule #1." That's it. See, I told you - 15 seconds and you did it. We'll come back to this later. Now let's move on.

Many people don't think about estate planning until it is too late. Too often, attorneys will get a call from a prospective client that may go like this. Let's suppose Joe calls me and says, "My mother has finally gotten to the point where she cannot handle her affairs. She is just not able to even understand what bank accounts she has, and she doesn't even recognize her close family. So I need to get a document for her to sign so that I can handle her affairs." I have to tell this client, "The document to which you are referring is called a 'Durable Power of Attorney.' In that document, your Mom could appoint you as her 'agent' so that you have the power to handle her financial affairs such as writing checks. "Yes, that is exactly what I need," Joe interjects. Then to the disappointment of Joe,

STEVE H. HORNSTEIN, ESQ., CPA, LL.M., CFP®

I continue with the following: "It appears that it is too late. You indicated that your Mother does not understand the nature of her assets nor who her family members are. Under the Probate Code in California and many other states too, this means that your Mother does not have the capacity to sign a Power of Attorney, nor any other important estate planning documents. Indeed, it may be that your Mother should sign a Power of Attorney, and also other important estate planning documents, such as a Will, a Trust, a Deed to real estate to put her real property into her Trust, an Assignment of Interest to put other property into the Trust, a Health Care Power of Attorney, and a Physician's Directive. But these documents must be signed by someone who is competent to sign, and based on what you told me, it is too late because your Mother is not competent to sign."

There are options for Joe and his mother. We could petition the court to appoint Joe as a "conservator" for his mother. But at a cost of perhaps $7,000 to $10,000 or more over time, it is much more expensive than the perhaps $100 to $300 cost if the Mother was able to sign a Power of Attorney. Thus, you can see that significant money can be saved and problems can be avoided by addressing important issues earlier rather than later. This is a general rule of financial planning, estate planning, as well as a general rule of life. Your retirement account will grow much larger when you start early. Life insurance is less expensive when you purchase it when you are younger, and before you get sick. And estate planning is generally less expensive when done early. Estate planning may become impossible if you wait too long.

We have prepared many estate plans under rushed circumstances. We have had many trust signings at the hospital. One of the first estate plans I prepared was for an individual who had weeks to live. While I was preparing the documents, he was running to financial institutions changing the beneficiaries. His goal was to stay alive long enough to get his estate plan completed. He died two hours after he signed the last document. Since then we have had many signings in hospitals under less than ideal circumstances. In one case, a lady was going in and out of consciousness the night before a risky surgery. When she would come to, she appeared to me to be competent. She knew who her family was and what her assets were. Thus she met the test under the California Probate Code for competency to sign an estate plan. And she wanted to sign. The notary suggested that we wait until the next day. I urged that we really should do the signing now. We did, and it's a good thing we did, as the next morning she died in surgery.

We went to the house of another client who had put off treatment for her colon cancer. If she hadn't procrastinated, most likely she would be with us today. She realized that she put off treatment for too long, but she decided that for her son, she was not going to put off her estate planning any longer. We had her signing at her house. She died a week later.

I don't give you these stories to depress you. And don't worry – getting an estate plan will not make you die any sooner! I give you these stories as a call to action. If you have been thinking of getting life insurance and you are healthy, then don't delay.

Get it now. If you have expenses for which you need to save and you have been thinking about getting a financial plan, then don't delay. Do it now. If you have been thinking of getting an estate plan, then don't delay. Get it now. I will say again, that as a general rule of life, doing things early is better than doing them later.

In this guide, I don't want to have a list of things NOT to do. After all, you don't get things done by NOT doing things. So now I will add to "Don't Procrastinate" the following: **"Do something today that moves you closer to your goals."** If one of your goals is to get an estate plan completed, then one of those "somethings" you can do is call your estate planning attorney, or call my office, or go to www.HornsteinTrust.com and start putting your thoughts down on an estate planning questionnaire. The point is, it won't get done if you don't take action. Once you get started, either by calling your existing attorney or calling my office or going to HornsteinTrust.com, you will have taken an infinite step forward towards checking off "Get an estate plan" on your list of things to finally get done. Remember at paragraph 1 of this Rule #1 where I asked to you to put the entry "Check Rule #1" in your calendar on a date one month from today? Now, one month from today, when you look at your calendar, if you still haven't moved forward on getting an estate plan, give yourself a swift kick in the butt (metaphorically speaking, as I don't want you to injure yourself), and then call my office and tell whoever answers, "I need help getting my estate plan done." We'll help you from there.

This brings us to our first rule of estate planning:

Recap of Rule #1: Don't Procrastinate or You or Your Family May End Up In Court! Generally, everything is less expensive when done early. Specifically, estate planning works out best when you do it early. And don't forget the add-on to this Rule: "Do something today that moves you closer to your goals."

Rule #2: Keep a signed copy of your Trust in an alternate location because if it gets lost, your family may have to go to court to prove what it said!

I can't stress enough the importance of having a signed copy of your documents in case the original documents are lost or can't be found. Also, make sure the people you have named as a successor Trustee of your Trust or Executor of your Will know where you are keeping your documents so that they can find them later! In case they can't be found, make sure your successor Trustee and Executor either have a signed copy or know who has a signed copy. My first case that went all the way to trial involved a procrastinator who put off getting an estate plan until shortly before he died. He wanted his assets to go one-half to his girlfriend of 20 years, and one-half to his son. However, he was a double procrastinator in that although he had been separated from his wife for thirty years, he hadn't gotten around to finalizing his divorce. Yes, he was still married and under the California Probate Code, if he died without a Will, his estate would go one-half to his wife, and one-half to his son. So, he prepared a complete estate plan leaving his assets one-half to his girlfriend and one-half to his son. Unfortunately, when he died, for some yet to be explained reason, his Trust was missing from his estate planning book. The other documents were there, including his Will, Powers of Attorney for Management of Property and for Health Care, and his Physician's Directive, but not his Trust. We thought that perhaps he took it to work to make a copy of it or show to a friend. We contacted his former employer to find out if perhaps he left the Trust in his desk, but he hadn't. We will likely never know what happened to it. Regardless, we didn't have it. When the original document is lost, under the California Probate Code, it is presumed to have been destroyed and revoked. However, he had two pieces of real property that he had deeded to the Trust and were therefore still owned by the Trust. In such situations, the procedure is to go to court to determine the existence of the Trust and its terms.

The attorney who drafted the Trust had a copy of the Trust in his computer so he printed it and petitioned the court to deem that unsigned copy be treated as an original. The wife had to be given notice of the hearing. She was given notice, and when neither she nor anyone else showed up to challenge the petition, the judge granted the petition to treat the unsigned copy of the Trust as the original, leaving the assets one-half to the girlfriend and one-half to the son.

I got involved with the case when the wife's attorneys petitioned the court to overturn the ruling. The wife's attorneys claimed that their secretary miscalendared the hearing such that the attorneys didn't show up in court to object to the petition. I had a fax that indicated that the wife hadn't even hired the attorneys until after the hearing. So I was thinking, how in the world can the wife possibly think she is going to get the judge to withdraw his ruling? But the judge, wanting to err on the side of allowing people to be heard and have their day in court, he did withdraw his ruling! We were going to have a trial. If the copy of the Trust were treated as an original, the girlfriend would get the other half. But if the copy was not treated as an original, the wife would get it. The son would get half regardless but he was on the side of the wife, his mother. After all, it was likely that his mother would leave her assets to her son one day. The girlfriend had kids of her own who would likely be the beneficiaries of her estate plan rather than her boyfriend's son. So it was a battle between, the wife from whom the decedent had been separated for 30 years and the girlfriend with whom he had been for 20 years. A nastier battle could hardly be envisioned.

The day of trial came. Incidentally, although I had gotten a good grade in my trial advocacy class in law school, this was my very first day of trial ever in a real court of law. When we walked into court, I saw three attorneys standing before this judge. Each of the attorneys had their head down. One by one, the judge pointed his finger at them and imposed sanctions against them in the amounts of $300 each. Although I walked in during the middle of this public shaming such that I hadn't seen the whole proceeding, it was apparent to me that these three attorneys had been ordered to provide to the court something that was impossible for them to provide. Yet here they were, three attorneys, likely with far more experience than I had, being publically humiliated as well as fined hundreds of dollars each. Needless to say, I was terrified. When the appropriate opportunity arose, I asked the clerk if she could let the judge know that this was my first day of trial ever, and that if there was any procedure I should follow that I was not following, it was because this was my first day of trial ever, and not because I was disrespecting the court.

With that, I felt calmer. I was ready. After all, I had the notary who notarized the Trust as a witness at the Trial. I had a declaration from the attorney who drafted the Trust, and I had the copy of the Trust. I thought, this case is a slam dunk. How could the wife even think she would have a chance? But when I presented the copy of the Trust as an exhibit at the Trial, the Judge asked me, "How do I know that this is a copy of the Trust that he signed?" I answered, "In the ordinary course of business, the attorney who drafted the Trust would save the documents on his computer, and this is the last version of the Trust that is saved in his computer." The Judge asked me again, "Yes, but how do I know that this is the copy of the Trust that he signed?" I paused and thought to myself, "Is this déjà vu? Didn't I just answer this? Well, maybe he didn't hear me." So I answered again, speaking a little more slowly this time, "Well, in the ordinary course of business, the attorney who drafted the Trust would save the documents on his computer, and this is the last version of the Trust that is saved in his computer." To my chagrin, the Judge asked the same question a third time. I repeated my answer again, this time speaking more loudly. Was this judge hard of hearing? At the fourth time, I reflected upon how this copy of the Trust may not have been the one that he signed, and I realized, and I answered, "You're right, Your Honor. We don't know." After all, the attorney may have made changes to the Trust document, printed it for signing, and then closed the file without saving it, in which case the Trust that was in the attorney's computer was not the Trust that was printed and signed.

Indeed, this is what the Judge was thinking. Yes, the Judge's insight had been groomed by decades on the bench, and this, after all, was, well, I'll say it one last time, my first day of trial, ever. With that, the Judge tossed the copy of the Trust behind him and said, "OK, let's have a trial to determine what the Trust said." With that, over the next four days, we proceeded to call as witnesses the decedent's friends, family members, and the notary to prove that the intent of the decedent was to leave his assets one-half to the girlfriend and one-half to his son.

A trial takes on a life of its own. At one point, the wife's attorney asked my client how much she had received from an insurance policy, perhaps to show the judge that my client received enough already and in fairness, if there is a sliver of doubt, the balance should be split between the wife and the son. The girlfriend, my client, refused to answer, despite my pleading with her to answer. Apparently, the decedent had told her to never tell anyone how much she would receive in life insurance. The next morning, she told the judge the value of the life insurance policy she had received. But it was too late. The damage to her credibility was done. Later, my client was asked a question that she said she did not understand. My client had a strong accent and it was clear that English was a second language for her. She was born in the Philippines and her native tongue was Tagalog. I told the Judge that she did not understand the question. But the judge stated on the record that it was his belief that my client was intentionally refusing to answer. The Judge did not like my client, and that could not help our case. The trial ended after four days and we all went home to await the Judge's ruling.

A big envelope arrived in the mail a few weeks later, and the return address was "Los Angeles Superior Court." This was it, the fate of my client was in this envelope. I gathered my office to read it. It was a 27 page decision, detailed far beyond my expectation. This Judge didn't miss a thing. He was far from hard of hearing. He heard and considered every nuance of every witness and every document. In the end, he ruled that the decedent's assets shall go one-half to my client, the girlfriend, and one-half to the decedent's son. The wife would get nothing. Nevertheless, the Judge refused to rule on who the Trustee of the Trust would be, that is, who would be the person to administer the Trust and actually sell the properties in the Trust and then write the checks to the girlfriend and the son. An additional petition would be needed, or a settlement with the son. For now, however, the wife would be furious. I knew it. I didn't think she would be angry enough to file an appeal, but that is what she did.

More than a year and a half later, we walked into California Court of Appeals. This is a very different setting than the Superior Court. In Superior Court, there are crying children in the hallways. To the chagrin of judges, people walk into court dressed in jeans and sandals – not the attorneys of course, unless they want a hefty fine imposed on them. In Superior Court, it is not entirely uncommon to have bailiffs with guns come running down the hallway to escort screaming family members out of the building. In Superior Court, the benches outside the court room are cold, hard, and uncomfortable.

At the Court of Appeals, however, everyone is wearing a suit, and the suits appear to be more expensive than in Superior Court. There are no crying children. In fact, there are no witnesses at all. The appellate court reviews only what the judge at the *lower* court saw and heard, in order to determine if the *lower* court judge made the right decision. And here we were, the California Court of Appeals, a building with more Italian marble than many buildings in Italy. There was a panel of five judges hearing the appeal on our case, our case of an estranged and bitter wife having the fight of her life to keep a lady she didn't like from getting her husband's money.

A month later, we got another big envelope in the mail. How long had it been since this case started? Let's see. When the man died on December 29, 2003, I wasn't even engaged yet. We went to court for our four-day trial in October 2005, I was already back from my honeymoon. We walked into the Grand Court of Appeal in June 2007, and now it was July 2007 – over three and a half years later. Again, my office and I gathered around a big envelope and we opened it. Fortunately, we had won again.

But where were we with this case? We still didn't have a Trustee to administer the Trust. No one could sell the property. It would either be the girlfriend or the wife's son, and the son was still in this fight. Ultimately, we reached a settlement with the son, who was a real estate agent, that if my client could be Trustee, the son would get the listings on the two properties (one residential and one commercial). It took a long time to sell the properties. The son only sold the residential property. Since the commercial property wasn't sold in the given time, my client was able to hire another real estate agent. By the time the properties were sold and the assets distributed and the final tax returns filed at the end of 2009, I had two children of my own… and I had tried several more cases.

But during the course of this case, I kept coming back to that first day. If only we had a signed copy of the Trust… Back on that first day, when the Judge asked how we knew that that copy of the Trust is the one that was signed, if I could have answered, "Well, Your Honor, please look at the last second to last page, before the notary page, you'll see his signature right there." I could have rested my case right there, on day one, and there wouldn't have been an appeal. In fact, there probably wouldn't have been a trial at all. The case would have been over during the discussions before trial.

I happen to be a CPA in addition to being an attorney. When I prepare tax returns, I return to my clients their original documents that they give me to prepare their returns... after I scan them. Wouldn't it be a good idea to scan all of the Trust and estate planning documents so that if any documents are ever lost, we'll know exactly what the documents said and that these are the documents that were signed? Yes, that would be a good idea! Since then, I have always offered my clients the opportunity to have my office scan their signed documents and even put them on a CD or flash drive for them to perhaps give to their children or give to the person they named as a successor Trustee, since the person named as successor Trustee will need to have the Trust to administer it. At least, if they can't find the original Trust, they'll have a signed copy of it so that it should be a slam dunk to have the court rule that the signed copy be treated as if it were an original.

What about leaving your original Trust with your attorney? I once had a prospective client call my office. She wanted us to redo her Trust book, and they wanted her prior attorney to pay for it. I called back the prospective client to get more details as to this unusual request. Apparently, her attorney kept the original book containing her Trust, Will, Powers of Attorney, and other documents. I can understand why the attorney would want to keep the original books of his clients. After all, he would be more likely to get the Trust administration work when a client passed away, because his clients' families would have to call him as he was holding the original documents. Perhaps that attorney did not address the risk of what would happen if his office burned down and all of his clients' documents were lost. And that is exactly what happened! Unfortunately, for both the attorney and all of his clients, there was a fire in the attorney's office and all of his clients' estate planning documents were destroyed. I am assuming that this attorney did not also scan the documents and keep "signed" copies stored on his computer system. Of course, his computer system was probably destroyed too. Unless he backed up his computer system to the "cloud," his scanned copies would have been destroyed too. My stomach sinks at the thought of that.

To avoid such problems, I do not keep clients' original documents in my office. I give them to the client to take with them and I advise them of Rule #2:

> **Recap of Rule #2: Keep a signed copy of your Trust in an alternate location because if it gets lost, your family may have to go to court to prove what it said!.**

Rule #3: Don't leave the Fox guarding the Henhouse (that is, don't leave the Trust in the hands of someone who will receive more if the Trust does not exist.).

In another case, the family knew where the Trust was. It was in the refrigerator. But in this case the decedent was married to his second wife to was not a beneficiary of his Trust. His adult kids were the beneficiaries and his kids were not the kids of the wife. The decedent and his second wife lived together in the decedent's house at the time he died. Now she was the only resident of the home now that her husband had passed away. When the decedent's adult children came to the house to get the Trust, the wife wouldn't let them in. The California Probate Code provides that if a decedent has more than one child and there is no Trust or Will, the decedent's separate property assets goes one-third to the wife and two-thirds to the children of the decedent. The wife was getting nothing under the Trust but one-third of the assets if there was no Trust or Will, and as she was likely holding the Trust book containing the Trust and the Will, she had control over how much she would receive. I believe it is likely that the wife consulted with an attorney who informed her that she would get one-third if there is no Trust or Will, but nothing if there is a Trust. I believe the wife destroyed the Trust that was in the refrigerator. Maybe she cooked the Trust in the oven just to make use of all of the kitchen appliances.

It is difficult to think years ahead, but to have an effective estate plan, we must do so. The husband had set up a Trust and had funded it with his separate property in order to protect his children. However, no matter how careful he had been in setting up his Trust and properly funding it with his separate property, he could only ensure his children's protection if one day his children could actually get their hands on the Trust, or at the least a copy of it. At least if they had a copy, then if the original couldn't be found, the children could take the copy to court. However, the husband left his Trust in the house where he lived with his second wife, and there was no copy. While perhaps he trusted his wife, it is often a good idea to not even give others the opportunity to do the wrong thing, which leads us to Rule #3. This rule applies to more than just estate planning. After all, you certainly wouldn't leave the cookie jar unattended in your 4 year old child's room, would you? And isn't the entirety of absolutely everything you own more important than a few cookies?

Recap of Rule #3: Don't leave the Fox guarding the Henhouse (that is, don't leave the Trust in the hands of someone who will receive more if the Trust does not exist.).

Rule #4: Don't take the shortcut of simply adding your adult child to your bank accounts unless you have fully considered the risks.

We had a client come to our office with a problem. The IRS had levied her bank account and took over $10,000 out of it. But she didn't owe the IRS! She was current with her tax filing. The IRS hadn't sent her any notice that anything was wrong. So why had the IRS taken her money? It turns out that she took the estate planning shortcut of simply adding her son to her account so that if she should pass away, the account would go to her son, or if she should become incapacitated, incapable of handling her affairs, her son would be able to access the account for her. Sadly, sometime later, unbeknownst to her, her son had tax troubles and the IRS began to send notices to her son. Her son was unable to pay the IRS and eventually, the IRS got a lien on his assets. Since he was on her account, the IRS treated the account as his own, and the IRS took the money owed right out of her account!

A better way for the client to accomplish her estate planning objectives would have been to appoint her son as her agent in her Durable Power of Attorney for Management of Property and Financial Affairs. Then she could take that document to the bank and add her son as merely a "signer" on her account as her agent rather than as a co-owner of her account.

If the mother were to become incapacitated, the son would still be able to access the account and sign checks on her behalf. However, if the mother were to pass away, the Durable Power of Attorney would no longer be in operation. So that the son could access the account after the mother passed away, the mother should simply add the son as a "beneficiary" of the account with the bank, or if the son is not to be the beneficiary but merely be able to administer the account, the mother should put the account into her Trust and have the son as a successor Trustee of her Trust or perhaps add the son as a co-Trustee to act with the mother so that either one of them can access the account. Whether the son is on the account as an "agent" under a Durable Power of Attorney or as a "Trustee" of a Trust, the account does not "belong" to the son. Rather, the son would be a "fiduciary." That is, he would be acting in a "fiduciary capacity" with a legal obligation to use the funds for the benefit of the owner, his mother, and then, as the son is not the owner, the IRS would have no claim to that money to pay the son's debts. Although it is often so enticing to take shortcuts, let Rule #4 be a reminder to you that a shortcut may not be the best road to follow.Recap of Rule #4: Don't take the shortcut of simply adding your adult child to your bank account unless you have fully considered the risks. You will be better protected if you make your adult child your agent under your Durable Power of Attorney and add your child as a beneficiary to your bank account, or put your bank account into your Trust and make your child the Successor Trustee or current co-Trustee of your Trust.

Recap of Rule #4: Don't take the shortcut of simply adding your adult child to your bank account unless you have fully considered the risks. You will be better protected if you make your adult child your agent under your Durable Power of Attorney and add your child as a beneficiary to your bank account, or put your bank account into your Trust and make your child the Successor Trustee or current co-Trustee of your Trust.

Rule #5: Get written confirmation of the beneficiary(ies) on your accounts from all financial institutions for which you named beneficiaries.

Years ago, my office was hired to challenge a beneficiary designation that was on an insurance policy of my client's father. His father had prepared a change of beneficiary form to make the beneficiary on his life insurance policy his Trust. The prior beneficiary designation had named my client's sister as the 100% beneficiary. The circumstances were suspicious as to how the sister had become 100% beneficiary on that prior beneficiary designation, but regardless, the father had since changed the beneficiary to the Trust. Or had he?

The father's financial advisor assisted the father in faxing his beneficiary change form to the insurance company. The financial advisor then called the insurance company to confirm that they had received the fax changing the beneficiary. However, years later, when the father passed away, the son as Trustee of the Trust contacted the insurance company to collect the proceeds from the policy on behalf of the Trust, only to be told by the insurance company that the Trust was not the beneficiary! Insurance companies generally do not disclose who the beneficiary is, except to the actual beneficiary, and this insurance company was no different. But the Trustee knew it was likely the sister. So we filed a petition and notified the insurance company that the policy was the subject of litigation.

Unfortunately, when we questioned the financial advisor, he informed us that he had no written confirmation of the change of beneficiary from the insurance company. He said he had faxed the change of beneficiary form but did not have a fax confirmation from the fax machine showing that it had been sent. At the time the financial representative helped to communicate with the insurance company, he felt he had been very careful. After all, he had even followed up with a phone call to the insurance company to make sure they received his fax, and the representative at the insurance company had told him that indeed, the fax had been received. However, he had no record of the identity of that financial representative. Even if he had, we would still be at the mercy of that financial representative stating that he or she had received the new beneficiary designation, and it would be miraculous if he or she remembered all these years later.

We even had the actual change of beneficiary form signed by the father, the same form the financial advisor says he faxed to the insurance company. So, couldn't we just give it to the insurance company now? The insurance company had a policy that beneficiary designations had to be received while the owner of the policy was alive and now that was not possible. The odds of success were diming. We would have to prove to a judge that it was the father's intent to change the beneficiary and that he had directed his financial advisor to send the change of beneficiary form, and that the financial advisor had done so, but that the insurance company had lost the form. Proving all of this to a Judge was possible and we were ready to move forward in doing so. But settlement was preferable on our end, and that is what we did. The policy was over $300,000 and we settled with our client's sister and we filed the settlement with the court. The settlement was for my client's sister to receive $35,000 and no more. If we had litigated the case, the cost of litigation may likely have exceeded $35,000, so overall, it was a good settlement for my client. Of course, if we had written confirmation from the insurance company of the beneficiary designation it had on file, this case would likely have come to an end with a simple letter to our client's sister's attorney. This case taught us a big lesson, and that is our Rule #5.Recap of Rule #5: Get written confirmation of the beneficiary(ies) on your accounts from all financial institutions for which you named beneficiaries.

Recap of Rule #5: Get written confirmation of the beneficiary(ies) on your accounts from all financial institutions for which you named beneficiaries.

Rule #6: Don't push the boundaries of unusual provisions unless you are willing to take the risk that those provisions will be challenged or even litigated in court.

For some, education may be very important and some may wish to encourage their children to pursue higher education. This can be done through a Trust. For example, a college professor desiring that her daughter seek higher education could provide that her daughter receive 1/3 of the Trust estate upon her daughter receiving a bachelor's degree, then half of the balance upon her attaining a master's degree, and finally, the balance upon her daughter attaining a Ph.D. While some might call this plan "controlling from the grave," others call it a mother providing proper incentives to encourage her daughter to achieve all she can achieve. Again, it depends on your family situation. So long as the distribution plan is not against public policy, it should generally be upheld. One court even upheld a plan that provided that her daughter receive her inheritance only if she married a Jewish man. This was an Illinois case so we can't rely on such a provision being upheld in California. Such provisions as these might be viewed as against "public policy," which is a term with which judges have great latitude and view differently depending on the judge.

It is not uncommon for someone to desire that their children live in their house after they pass away. If a mother wanted her Trust to provide that her house remain in Trust for children to live in together for their lives, I would ask the mother about her children and their families. If it turns out that she has two daughters who are grown and married with children of their own, my next logical question would be, "Well, how big is your house?" If the mother lives in a castle, the provision may be just fine. But if the mother lives in 3,000 square foot house, and each of her daughters live in similarly sized houses of their own, it just may not make sense to expect her kids to leave their homes and move into it. Such a provision would be a lot to ask of both of her daughters and their husbands to sell their homes and move in together. While it might be nice for a mother to think of her daughters and their families all living together in harmony, before putting such a provision into a Trust, it has to be given great thought. I can foresee just one of the daughters moving in, and the other daughter suing her sister for rent or at least resenting her sister for getting a free place to live while the other one isn't. Certainly, your kids suing each other in court likely isn't your plan. Therefore, it is important to consider that the more you go out on a limb with unusual and hard to follow and hard to administer provisions, the more likely it is that such provisions may end up being litigated in court. Hence, Rule #6:

Recap of Rule #6: Don't push the boundaries of unusual provisions unless you are willing to take the risk that those provisions will be litigated in court.

Rule #7: Don't assume your children will get along just fine if they haven't always gotten along in the past (or even if they have gotten along in the past).

Sibling rivalry has been the subject of books, articles, and doctoral research projects. Even the bible addresses it. Here in this guide, it is one chapter, as it relates to estate planning. Indeed, sibling relationships as it relates to estate planning could also be a whole book, even a series of books. Here, I've got one chapter, and I will try to keep it as brief as necessary.

I had a case several years ago in which I was hired by a co-Trustee of her father's Trust to help with administering and settling it. Her father had made her a co-Trustee with her brother. In this case, it appeared likely that she had experienced some differences of opinion with her brother while growing up. With a strong act of penmanship, their father was going to make them work together after he was gone. It didn't work out well. Practically upon their father's passing, the brother was ready to get the house cleaned out and listed for sale. The sister, my client, on the other hand, wanted to carefully go through every picture and piece of paper and reflect on better times. Perhaps a few months could have been reasonable to get the house listed for sale. The sister may have taken a year. The brother may have taken a week. It was apparent that the brother moved too fast. It was equally apparent that the sister moved too slow.

In the ensuing dispute, he changed the locks to the house so she couldn't get in. She hired a locksmith and sent him the bill. Eventually, we ended up in court seeking to have the brother removed as Trustee, and I was going to keep my client moving at a reasonable pace. Eventually, we settled the case by agreeing on a time schedule of events to occur such as cleaning out the house, splitting up personal property, selling the house, paying expenses, and such. The judge ordered that my attorney-client trust account would hold the Trust bank account and no checks would be written without approval from both brother and sister. The Trust house got sold, property divided, house sold, proceeds split, and the Trust got settled in a reasonable period of time. But having the two of them as co-Trustees caused extra expense and a great deal of tension between the siblings. I expect the father would have been saddened to hear his son tell his sister outside the courtroom that he would never speak with her again. The sister started crying. I cried too. It was a shame and it didn't have to happen this way.

Had the family dynamics been reviewed at the time the father prepared his Trust, a better plan could have been developed rather than having the two siblings as co-trustees – perhaps having an independent trustee; perhaps having another person act as a tie-breaker (a "trust protector") if disputes arose; perhaps discussing with his kids the issues of being a trustee; perhaps a meeting with his kids and his attorney; perhaps being more specific in the terms of the trust to leave less discretion to the brother and sister. Instead, unfortunately, the father forced his kids to work together when the time came that the father wouldn't be there to resolve problems.

The key is that before you finalize the terms of your trust, it is important to consider the personalities and emotions of your children and how they get along. It also couldn't hurt to talk about this with your attorney who has probably seen these issues arise before.

Every so often, in certain family situations, everything can work out just fine, despite how otherwise poorly someone may have set up their estate plan. One parent had left her assets equally to her five adult children, but had left one of her five children on an account with her that contained a substantial amount of money. She had expected that this child would split the account equally with his other four siblings, and he did just that, even though legally, he could have just kept all of the money in that account. He shared his mother's motto: "Share and share alike." Everyone got along just great, and there were no problems whatsoever. But what if he thought that sharing wasn't such a good idea? His siblings would likely have sued him and the parent arguably would be partially to blame for setting up this situation.

I had another case where indeed, the sister didn't think sharing was a good idea. She kept the money in which the mother had put her on the account. Her brother sued her. I was hired by the sister to defend her and we ended up in a four day jury trial. There are no jury trials in probate court, but this case had been filed in civil court. I came into the case late in the case as several prior attorneys had backed out. I took the case because I believed in my client, and I thought we could win. We almost did.

Their father had died years prior, and the brother had been estranged from the mother for years, but reconciled in the year preceding their mother's passing. The mother's house was held in joint tenancy with the daughter, which meant that when the mother passed, the house would go to her daughter. In the year prior to the mother's passing, the mother had consulted with an attorney regarding changing her estate plan to leave her assets equally to her daughter and her son. But she never actually changed her estate plan. That attorney testified against my client stating that it was my client who influenced her mother to not make any changes and to leave the house held in joint tenancy. The daughter apparently made statements to her brother that led the brother to believe that his sister was agreeing to share with him the house when their mother died. When the time came, the sister denied ever agreeing to such a thing. So the brother sued his sister alleging an oral agreement to share the proceeds from the sale of the house she inherited from their mother.

At trial, in addition to the mother's attorney testifying against my client, the brother himself testified. Of course he was biased in favor of himself, but he came across as very believable. He testified that his mother had told him that she wanted the house to be split between his sister and him, and that his sister had agreed to do so. My client testified that their mother had told her that she wanted the house to go 100% to her. Certainly, one of them must be lying, yes? At first, I thought one of them was lying. But towards the end of the trial, I came to believe that they were both telling the truth. I explained this to the jury in my closing argument.

See, in the testimony of both brother and sister, it came out that the mother never stated her wishes in the presence of both of them. So it was entirely plausible that when the brother, her son, was not around, she told her daughter that she wanted her to have 100% of the house. Likewise, when the sister, my client, was not around, the mother told her son that she wanted him to have one-half of the house with his sister. Why would the mother tell each of her children different things?

I had a hypothesis that answered this question. It came out in the brother's testimony that he became estranged from his mother because she told him something he didn't want to hear. What she had told him was that she didn't like his wife. At hearing that, he left and didn't see or talk to his mother again for ten years.

Here is my hypothesis that I argued to the jury: The mother had lost a relationship with her son for ten years. At the time, she probably feared she would never see him again. Well, by the time the son came back into her life, she was 90 years old and very sick. If one of her children left for ten years at that point, she would surely never see him or her again. But now, at 90 years old, she had both of her children in her life, and she wasn't going to risk losing either of them again. I argued to the jury that she had decided that in order to make sure that no one would leave her for hearing something they didn't want to hear, she would tell everyone close to her exactly what they wanted to hear. So, she told her son that he wanted him to have 50% of the house because that's what her son wanted to hear. And she told her daughter that she wanted her to have 100% of the house because that's what her daughter wanted to hear. Conveniently, she never talked about what she wanted when both of them were with her. The mother was smart. She knew exactly what she wanted, and that was that both her son and daughter be with her for the rest of her life.

But what did she really want with regard to her estate plan? We will never know, I told the jury. Quite possibly, she didn't care who got the house. But what we do know is that she left her house in joint tenancy with her daughter. That we know for sure. I also argued the "statute of frauds," which is a legal doctrine that agreements regarding real property must be in writing. The judge let me argue this to the jury but ruled against me on it absolutely applying because the brother argued that the agreement was to share the "proceeds" from sale of the real estate, not the real estate itself. That was potentially an appealable issue if the jury found for the brother. In the end, the jury did find for the brother. Although two jurors of the twelve jurors sided with the daughter, we needed four of them.

A trial takes on a life of its own, and some of that life is often not within your control. You just can't be sure enough who you will get on your jury. You also can't completely control your witnesses or parties. In this case, the brother had also sued the sister's husband because after the mother died, the sister deeded half of the house to her husband. At first, I represented both the sister and her husband, but by the time of the trial, I represented only the sister. This could have worked to our advantage in that the husband could speak to the jury directly and also question the witnesses himself, potentially having another opportunity to sway the jury. Unfortunately for my client, the sister, her husband didn't come across well to the jury and it didn't work in our favor.

Another such moment outside of the control of my client or myself occurred during the voir dire process. Voir dire is the process by which members of the jury are questioned by the attorneys who are given the opportunity to dismiss a limited number of jurors for any reason, or any of them "for cause," or when there is a good reason they should not be on the jury. During voir dire, a prospective juror that I had hoped would be on our jury panel was asked if there was any reason he thought he couldn't be impartial. He asked to speak privately with the Judge. The Judge invited the attorneys to hear what he had to say outside the presence of the other jurors. The juror stated that during lunch when I had left the lunch room (I had gone to my car to get my story board exhibits to show the jury in my opening statement), the juror had witnessed the person sitting next to me in the courtroom screaming at my co-counsel, and it left him with a very bad impression of that person such that he didn't feel he could be impartial if it turned out that that person he saw screaming was a party to the case. It turned out that the person he saw screaming was the husband of my client and was integral to my client's case. So we had to say goodbye to a juror I had felt would have otherwise been one of the best for my client.

In the end, of the jurors that remained, we didn't have enough of them siding with my client. It is another reminder that you should never be so certain that others will see things the way you do. Remember that there are Democrats that you will never convince to vote for a Republican, and there are Republicans that you will never convince to vote for a Democrat. Always recognize the possibility that others won't agree with you. That would be a good rule also, but the real reason for this chapter is how we got into these cases in the first place, which brings us to Rule #7, which should always be considered if you have kids.

Recap of Rule #7: Don't assume your children will get along just fine if they haven't always gotten along in the past (or even if they have gotten along in the past).

Rule #8: Fund your Trust with what should be in your Trust... But don't put into your Trust what shouldn't be in your Trust.

> "A probate won't be needed if you have a trust *and properly fund your assets into your Trust.* And this may be the reason you are reading this guide now – to avoid a probate! Therefore, funding your Trust is extremely important, as a probate can be quite expensive."

It is important to remember that your Trust only governs what it owns. If there is an asset or account that is not in the Trust (and the account does not have a valid beneficiary form on file with the financial institution), it will be in your estate when you pass. Being in your estate, it will be governed by your Will. If you have our firm prepare a complete estate plan for you, your Trust book will include a "pourover" Will. It is called a "pourover" Will because the Will pours over into your Trust anything you leave out of your Trust, and then it is your Trust that provides who will be the ultimate beneficiaries. Your Trust can also provide conditions that must occur in order for beneficiaries to receive their distributions. Such conditions could be reaching a certain age or graduating from college.

In California, if your Will governs more than $150,000 of property, or real estate of a lesser amount, your Will may have to be probated in court. As discussed in Part 1, "probate" is the court process to determine the validity of a Will and to give creditors an opportunity to file claims and ask the judge to pay them before allowing your beneficiaries to be paid. I often use the example of a house. The only person who can sign a deed to the house is the owner. So if the owner dies, who can sign the deed to the owner's beneficiaries? No one. That's when a probate will be needed to fill the gap in the "chain of title" between one person owning property and the owner's beneficiaries owning property. That gap will be filled by the Order of the judge in the probate court, ordering that the property is now owned by the new owners, your beneficiaries. States other than California may have different values of assets requiring a probate. If you have assets in more than one state that have not been properly funded into your Trust, your Will may need to be probated in every state in which you have property. A probate won't be needed if you have a trust *and properly fund your assets into your Trust.* This may be the reason you are reading this guide now – to avoid a probate! Therefore, funding your Trust is extremely important, as a probate can be quite expensive.

In California, the probate fees are statutorily set by the Probate Code based on the value of the estate, and the court will appoint a probate referee to value the estate in order to determine the fees that the court will order. These are the attorney fees. Currently, the fees are 4% of the first $100,000, 3% of the next $100,000, 2% of the next $800,000, and there is a sliding scale for larger estates. These fees are based on the gross value of the estate, not on the net value. So if you have a $1 million house with a $990,000 mortgage, the probate fees are based on the $1 million, not on the $10,000 of equity. For a $1 million probate, the probate fees will be at least $23,000. The court could order that "extraordinary fees" be paid on top of that if there is additional work for which the court agrees the attorney should be paid. That is just the probate fee. Further, the executor (if there is a will) or administrator (if there is not a will) is entitled to a fee equal to the probate fees. So that would mean an additional $23,000 on a $1 million estate. If the executor or administrator is the sole beneficiary, they will likely choose not to take the fee, because the fee is taxable income. But if the executor or administrator is not the sole beneficiary, he or she will be able to get a fee in addition to his or her beneficial share.

On top of these fees, there will also be costs such as the court filing fee and the cost to publish the probate in the newspaper. The probate must be published in order to give creditors notice of the probate so that they can file claims with the court to be paid from the estate before any money is released to beneficiaries. The probate referee appointed by the court will also have to be paid to appraise the property in order to calculate how much money is available to pay creditors and to calculate the probate fees. After everything, a probate of a $1 million estate in California may cost in the neighborhood of $25,000 or more and it could take a year or longer; add another $23,000 if the executor or administrator fee is not waived. While I have completed probates in less than a year, I once had a probate that took over eight years! Spending all of this time and money can be avoided if your property is properly funded into your

Living Trust.

Again, your Trust only governs what it owns. If an asset is not in your Trust, and has no valid beneficiary designation attached to it, it will be governed by your Will when you pass, and it may then require a court proceeding such as a probate to get the asset into your Trust. Thus it is important to actually fund your Trust with assets that should be in your Trust. But it is just as important to NOT fund into your Trust certain types of assets that should NOT be in your Trust. Whether the type of asset is a "Qualified" or "Non-qualified" asset will determine whether you should fund the asset into your Trust or whether instead you should have a beneficiary form on file with the financial institution. I will refer to "accounts" rather than "assets" here because this discussion typically involves accounts that are held at a financial institution or insurance company. While in reality a "qualified" account is one that is governed by ERISA and thus includes a 401(k) but not an IRA, for the purposes of this discussion as it is relevant to your estate plan I am going to simplify my definition. To make this easy to remember and useful to you in your estate planning, you can think of a "qualified" account as an account that is "qualified" under the Internal Revenue Code to receive tax-deferred or tax-free treatment. For estate planning purposes, you can think of qualified accounts as accounts such as IRAs and Roth IRAs, 401(k)s, 403(b)s, and other such tax-deferred or tax-free accounts for which you may not pay taxes on the earnings each year. Sometimes, cash value life insurance policies and annuities may also be treated as "qualified" accounts. You can think of these as "qualified accounts" because they qualify under the Internal Revenue Code for tax-deferred or tax-free treatment. You can consider all other accounts as being "non-qualified." If you receive a Form 1099 showing your income you earned in an account, such that you have to include that income on your income tax return for the year, then that account is a "non-qualified" account.

What to do with "Non-qualified" accounts (e.g. non-retirement accounts):

We recommend that you actually fund non-qualified accounts into your Trust. For example, you should go to the bank and "title" the account in the name of your Trust. Then the account is said to be "funded" into your Trust. To fund your non-qualified accounts such as a bank account into your Trust, you will take your Certification of Trust (in Section 1 of your Trust book)

> **"We recommend that you actually fund non-qualified accounts into your Trust."**

to your bank and tell the banking representative that you set up a Living Trust and you want to fund the Trust with your bank account. For other accounts such as your brokerage account, you can request a change of account form or speak with your financial representative regarding the forms needed to make the Trust the owner of your accounts. We can assist you with transferring your other assets to your Trust and you can call us from your bank if needed and we can walk you and your banker or financial representative through the process.

What to do with "Qualified" accounts (e.g. IRAs, 401(k)s, insurance policies, and annuities):

For "Qualified" accounts, you should fill out a beneficiary form and have the form on file with the financial institution. Call the financial institutions where you have such accounts,

> **"For 'Qualified' accounts, you should fill out a beneficiary form and have the form on file with the financial institution."**

and request that they send you a "Change of Beneficiary Form." Qualified accounts should NOT be titled into your Trust because changing the account owner on a retirement account may be treated as a withdrawal by the IRS such that your retirement account is taxable upon the change of ownership, even if the owner is simply changed to a trust of which you and your spouse are the owners and trustees. If you are married, you can make your spouse the primary beneficiary and your Trust the contingent beneficiary. If the spouse is not the primary beneficiary, your spouse may need to sign a "spousal consent" in order for your beneficiary designation to be valid.

For your non-qualified accounts at a bank, your bank should be able to put your bank account into your Trust and allow you to keep the same account number. However, your banker may tell you that in order to fund your bank account into your Trust, the banker has to close your current account and open a new one in the name of your Trust. This could be inconvenient because you may have set up automatic deposits and withdrawals and bill payments for your account. It could likely be a hassle to set these up all over again. If this is the case, perhaps speak with another banker to see if it is possible to keep your same account number but simply change the owner of the account to your Trust. In my experience, I have found that banks have less problems keeping the account number the same if you are the only one on your current account and you are the only trustee of your Trust. The same result should apply if you and your spouse are the only signers on your old account and you and your spouse are the only trustees of your Trust. On the other hand, I sometimes find that the bank may be more likely to want to close your account and open a new account if the signers are changing, such as if you are the only one on your current account, but both you and your spouse are the Trustees of your Trust and thus, the signers on your new account. In this case, if your banker says you have to open a new account, consider asking your banker to add your spouse to your account and then "convert" the account to be owned by your Trust. If ultimately, the banker says they can't do it and they need to open a new account and transfer your funds from your old account in your name to your new account in the name of your Trust, and that is not good for you, then there is another solution.

Your alternate solution is to simply **add a beneficiary to your bank account and make that beneficiary your Trust.** You do this by asking the bank for a "POD" ("Pay on Death") Form. For an account with an investment firm that holds securities such as stocks and bonds and mutual funds, the form is called a

"TOD" ("Transfer on Death") Form. The logic is that you "pay" money that is in a bank account but you "transfer" securities that are in an investment account. On a POD or TOD form, you can provide that the primary beneficiary is your spouse (if you are married), and the contingent beneficiary is your Trust. If you are not married, then you may simply make your Trust your primary beneficiary.

Funding your non-qualified accounts into your Trust is better than adding a beneficiary with a POD or TOD form because it is more difficult to be certain that the beneficiary is actually added than it is to be certain that the account is funded into your Trust. If the Trust is merely a "beneficiary" of your account, your statements will not likely indicate this. Your bank statements often do not show that the POD beneficiary form is on file at the bank. Also sometimes, when one bank takes over another bank, these POD forms may be lost. On the other hand, if you actually fund your account into your Trust, your bank statements will show your Trust as the owner so you will know it is funded into your Trust. If you use a POD or TOD form rather than funding your account into your Trust, please be sure to get written confirmation from the financial institution that this has been done. Keep that written confirmation in an important place, such as with your Trust documents.

A Hornstein Trust book includes forms showing your intention to fund, and your assignment of, your non-qualified assets into your Trust. Your qualified accounts will be listed on a schedule of "non-Trust assets" showing your intent to not fund those accounts into your Trust.

A Hornstein Trust book includes a carefully drafted document called a "Declaration of Intent" to fund your non-qualified assets into your Trust. Our "Declaration of Intent" specifically excludes qualified accounts for a good reason. In the course of litigation regarding the settling of a Trust prepared by another firm, we went through a 20 hour mediation and then binding arbitration. In this case, the decedent had designated beneficiaries on his IRA that differed from the beneficiaries on his Trust. At the arbitration, the Judge ruled that an IRA was to be distributed pursuant to the terms of the Trust rather than the beneficiaries he designated on his IRA because the Declaration of Intent prepared by that law firm said that all assets were intended to be held in Trust. The Declaration of Intent failed to exclude qualified assets. With a Hornstein Trust book, the Declaration of Intent specifically excludes qualified accounts such as IRAs.

Rolling qualified accounts into "stretch IRAs" to achieve tax benefits:

Your beneficiaries may be able to roll qualified accounts into another IRA to achieve tax benefits. As qualified accounts are generally not taxed until the funds are taken out of the account, there are tax benefits to be gained by your beneficiaries continuing to defer taking withdrawals until later. Such an IRA is called a "stretch IRA" because the beneficiary can "stretch" the time for taking mandatory distributions from the IRA and thus having it taxed. With proper planning, your beneficiaries may be able to "stretch" the tax benefits of your IRAs by being able to take funds out of the IRA over a term of years well beyond your passing. You should speak with your attorney, your financial advisor, or your tax advisor, or our office regarding the tax and other implications affecting your beneficiaries rolling over the inherited funds from your qualified accounts into their own IRAs or Inherited IRAs.

Generally, a beneficiary of an IRA or a 401(k) account may be able to roll over the account into their own IRA or an "inherited IRA" and continue being able to defer having to take funds out of the account and have it subject to income tax. The beneficiary may be able to take elect to take funds out over a term of years based on IRA tables using either the beneficiary's age or the age of the decedent, depending on the age at which the decedent passed. A Trust doesn't necessary have an "age" so when the Trust is a beneficiary, the financial institution may be able to "look through" the Trust to see who the beneficiaries are. Based on the information and language in the Trust, beneficiaries "of the Trust" may be able to roll over the accounts to their own IRAs or inherited IRAs. However, the age of the oldest beneficiary may have to be used to determine the withdrawal rate for all of the beneficiaries thereby causing the time of the deferral to be shorter than if the younger beneficiary were specified as the beneficiary of the qualified account rather than the Trust. Still, we often find that a somewhat shorter deferral period is a small price to pay in order to get the desired distribution among beneficiaries. After all, having the Trust as a beneficiary will allow you to specify that if a beneficiary were to pass, the deceased beneficiary's share should go to that deceased beneficiary's issue. You can also specify that a beneficiary must wait until they are a specified age before receiving their distribution outright. You may not be able to make these specific choices without having your Trust as the beneficiary.

The technique of "stretching IRAs" can be a complicated area. You should speak with your financial advisor, tax advisor, or our office, regarding the tax implications affecting your beneficiaries rolling over the inherited funds from your qualified accounts into their own IRAs or Inherited IRAs. It is also important that you discuss with your advisors each year to make sure your Trust is properly funded and that your beneficiary designations are proper and up to date.

Recap of Rule #8: Fund your Trust with what should be in your Trust...But don't put into your Trust what shouldn't be in your Trust.

Rule #9: Think a generation up as well as a generation down.

People generally think of estate planning as arranging their affairs so that their children can easily inherit their assets without unnecessary complications and without having to go through an expensive probate and without having to pay unnecessary expenses and taxes. However, generally speaking, most of the clients I see are the surviving children rather than the deceased parents. In fact, I am quite certain that no deceased person has ever hired me. It is the surviving children who come to see me. Too often they say, "My parent just passed away and I can't find an estate plan. I think they didn't have one. What do I do now?"

This is why I say when you are doing your estate planning, also think about from whom you may be inheriting property one day and consider the question, "Do these people from whom I might be inheriting have an estate plan?" If not, then it is you who may bear the burden of a costly probate or other court involvement.

I often tell people, **"If you don't know where your parent's or adult child's estate plan is, they probably don't have one."** People ask me, "Well, I am pretty sure my parents don't have an estate plan. But how do I ask them about it?" I recognize that it is a difficult conversation, or awkward at

> **"If you don't know where your parent's or adult child's estate plan is, they probably don't have one."**

the least, but it is a very important conversation. I think a good way to bring it up is to give your parents a copy of your estate plan and say, "Here is a copy of my estate plan to keep with your important papers in case it us ever needed, such as if the original should become lost. By the way, where do you keep your estate plan?" Your parents will likely either tell you where their estate plan is, or they'll be surprised that their child got an estate plan before they did. Hopefully see that as a call to action. They may not get their estate plan immediately, but at least you will have planted the seed. Perhaps, tell them about the website HornsteinTrust.com, or maybe take out your cell phone and go to HornsteinTrust.com and show them how easy it is to get started. Ultimately, you can only do so much. At least raise the issue and offer to help.

Recap of Rule #9: Think a generation up as well as a generation down.

Rule #10: Update your estate plan, including beneficiary designations, when you get married, divorced or a child is born.

Is your ex-spouse the beneficiary of your retirement plan?

When you get married, you have to have your spouse as the primary beneficiary on your qualified retirement accounts that are governed by ERISA unless the spouse signs a consent. ERISA is the Employee Retirement Income Security Act of 1974. But if you should happen to get a divorce, and you don't update your beneficiary designation, guess who gets the qualified plan when you pass away? If you guessed "your ex-spouse," you guessed right. If you remarry, and leave your ex-wife as beneficiary, your wife and our ex-wife maybe duking it out in

> **Make sure your beneficiary designations are up to date and the way you want.**

court. After all, your current spouse had to have signed a consent to not be the primary beneficiary. But that still might not prevent your ex-spouse from challenging that. Further, if only your ex-wife files a beneficiary claim form, your ex-spouse will likely get the funds. After all, the financial institution may not know you got divorced and remarried. According to their records, they show your ex-spouse as beneficiary, and they received a claim form from the named beneficiary. When your ex-spouse gets the money, your current spouse would have to sue your ex-spouse for a return of the funds. To avoid this mess, **make sure your beneficiary designations are up to date and the way you want.**

This area of law gets tricky as some retirement plans, such as 401(k)s are governed by ERISA, but other plans such as IRAs are not. As you may be uncertain as to which of your accounts are governed by ERISA and which are not, I suggest not relying on the distinction. If possible, it is best to keep your beneficiary designations up to date and always get the consent of your spouse if your spouse is not the primary beneficiary. The more you remove the potential to have your estate plan challenged, the more likely your estate plan will not be challenged.

Children should be specifically identified within your Trust. In Rule #8 regarding the funding of your Trust, I discussed that your children may be able to roll over an inherited qualified account into their own IRA or an inherited IRA. But if the Trust is the beneficiary of your IRA and your children are the beneficiaries of your Trust, your children can only roll over the account into their own "stretch IRA" if your children are specifically identified in the Trust. Therefore, whenever a new child is born, it is important to update your Trust to specifically identify your children. A Hornstein Trust always specifically identifies the children of the creator (the "Settlor").

What if you forget to update your estate plan when you get married? When you get married, it is very important that you update your estate plan to provide that you are married. Under the Probate Code in California, if your estate plan does not provide for your current spouse, the spouse is deemed to be an unintentionally omitted spouse, and your spouse will receive what is called his or her "omitted spousal share" of your separate property. The amount of that share depends on how many children you have. If you have no children, the omitted spousal share is 100% of your separate property. If you have one child, the omitted spousal share is 50% of your separate property. If you have more than one child, the omitted spousal share is one-third of your separate property. Therefore, whenever you get married, it is very important that you update or restate your estate plan to provide that you are now married. In fact, whenever you have a big life event, it is a good idea to review your estate plan and make sure that it reflects your wishes and discuss with your attorney whether it needs to be updated.

Recap of Rule #10: Update your estate plan, including beneficiary designations, when you get married, divorced or a child is born.

Rule #11: Have the caregiver sign a contract that as a condition of employment, he or she will not marry your mother or father.

An elderly client of ours had a girlfriend who was more mentally witty than he, and he was concerned that she may convince him to marry her one day. So I had an idea. We gathered a number of his family members and friends to witness him sign a document that stated that he had no intention of changing his estate plan and had no intention of getting married, and if he should change his estate plan or get married without giving everyone in the room sixty days notice, the changes to his Trust and also the marriage shall be deemed to be the product of undue influence. I mentioned this idea to other attorneys at my monthly estate planning group meeting, and many of them nodded in approval saying "That's a good idea." Nevertheless, as I have since learned, that won't work, at least with respect to invalidating the marriage.

We had a case in 2012 that went to a four-day trial. A husband and wife, let's call them Joe and Wendy, had been married for 61 years. They had no children, but they went to a restaurant every day for lunch and dinner for perhaps 30 years. They got to know the waitresses very well. So, in their Trust, they left the house to one of the waitresses and everything else to another waitress. The "everything else" vanished quickly, but we sought to protect the house for the benefit of the waitress who was to get the house.

Another acquaintance of Joe and Wendy came down to take

care of them, in their old age, to be their caregiver. Let's call the caregiver "Beth" or simply "Caregiver." Well, within a couple of weeks of Caregiver's arrival to take care of Joe and Wendy, Joe and Wendy's Trust was amended to leave everything to Beth. Then a couple of weeks later, Wendy died. And one of their dogs died, or rather was put down, and another dog ran away. Then 18 days after Joe lost his wife of 61 years, Caregiver took Joe to Las Vegas and married him! Caregiver and Joe checked the box on the application for a marriage license to have the marriage be deemed a "confidential" marriage. The marriage really wasn't confidential, as Caregiver told everyone, but by checking the box and declaring that they met the requirements for a "confidential" marriage, under the law, the marriage was deemed to be a confidential marriage. Then three months and seventeen days later, Joe died.

Before Caregiver could sell the house, but after she cleaned out the bank accounts, we were hired by the waitress who would have gotten the house, to challenge the amendment to Joe and Wendy's Trust. We also challenged the validity of the marriage between Joe and Caregiver. It was important to challenge the marriage because under the California Probate Code, if there is no estate plan that is drafted after the marriage, the Probate Code assumes that the spouse was simply forgotten unintentionally, as no one would want to leave their spouse nothing, right? So Caregiver as the omitted spouse could possibly get her "spousal share" under the Probate Code, which in this case, since there were no children, would be 100% of the Joe's assets.

On the first day of trial, the Judge stated that we could not challenge the marriage because of the Pryor vs. Pryor case. This case involved the famous comedian, Richard Pryor. Unbeknownst to Richard Pryor's children, he had gotten married several years before his death in a confidential marriage. So when Mr. Pryor died, his wife would receive her spousal share of Mr. Pryor's assets, which, in that case, since he had more than one child, would be one-third of his estate. Mr. Pryor's daughter challenged the marriage stating that her father was ill and that he was unduly influenced to get married. The daughter lost. The Judge ruled that the only one who could challenge the marriage was Mr. Pryor, and since he was unable to challenge the marriage, as he was deceased, the marriage stood, and his spouse got one-third.

At our trial involving the marriage to Joe and Beth, the Judge cited the Pryor case and said we could not challenge it. Only Joe could, and he wasn't with us anymore. We argued that we weren't contesting the marriage due to undue influence, but rather because Joe and Beth didn't follow the formalities required to have a confidential marriage. To have a confidential marriage, the couple had to live together as husband and wife, and here, we argued, they lived together as caregivee and caregiver.

Beth's attorney countered that there is no requirement as to how long Joe and Beth had to live together as husband and wife, so even if they did not live together as husband and wife for the first 17 days after his wife of 61 years passed away, if they lived together as husband and wife on the day they got married on the 18th day after his wife of 61 years passed away, that's enough to live together as husband and wife.

We further argued that the policy of allowing a confidential marriage was so that if a couple had a child, and everyone thought that child's parents were married, that child should not be shamed due to a public marriage after the child's birth. Yes, although this is more commonplace now, that was the purpose of a confidential marriage, and in our case, Joe and Beth had no children.

Regardless, the Judge held against us on the marriage issue. Beth had successfully married the person she was caring for, and I realized that my great idea wasn't so great. It won't work to gather friends and family around to witness someone's declaration that if he or she got married without giving his friends and family 60-days' notice, the marriage should be deemed to be the product of undue influence. Based to the Judge's ruling in the Richard Pryor case, it appears that won't work! We had planned to appeal this issue but it turned out that we won the case in full anyway, so there was no need to appeal. How we won, I will explain. However, I do believe there is a problem here in California and perhaps many other states too in that it is too easy for a caregiver to get away with horrible wrongdoing by marrying the person for whom he or she is caring through undue influence! The only way I currently see to prevent this wrongdoing on your parents is to get a conservatorship over your parents as soon as they become incapacitated, or to utilize contract law, that is, have the caregiver sign a contract that he or she won't marry your parents! Even then, I can't be certain this will work!

I am sure you are asking, "Well, how did you win the trial?" To understand, I need to explain that all of Joe's and Wendy's property was community property and they had an AB Trust, which is a type of Trust a married couple can have (see Rule #17). With an AB Trust, when one spouse passes, the Trust must be split into two trusts; the A Trust to hold the surviving spouse's share of the community property and the B Trust to hold the decedent's share of the community property. Thus, upon Wendy's death, Joe and Wendy's Trust containing all of their community property had to be split into two equal shares, Joe's survivor's Trust (the A part) over which Joe had complete control and Wendy's decedent's Trust (the B part), which became irrevocable upon Wendy's death, and thus was unable to be changed by Joe. If we could successfully argue that Joe and Wendy were not competent to sign the amendment, we could at least prevent Caregiver from getting anything from Wendy's decedent's Trust. Thus immediately after the Judge ruled the marriage was not contestable, I thought that we were fighting over only the property in Wendy's decedent's Trust, which was to hold one-half of Joe's and Wendy's property. I didn't yet see how to prevent Caregiver from getting all of the property in Joe's survivor's Trust as Joe didn't amend the Trust after he and Caregiver got married so Caregiver would be treated as an omitted spouse and would thus be entitled to her spousal share, which was ALL of Joe's survivor's Trust since he had no children.

However, to my client's good fortune, Beth tried a little too hard to improperly take all of Joe's and Wendy's property. What she did, obviously without the advice of counsel, is cause Joe (so we believe) to scribble on the back of another estate document, "I leave my dog Puddypots and all of my estate to my wife, Caregiver." I realized that, because of laws of which Caregiver and her attorney were obviously unaware, this was wonderful for my client!

In my closing argument, which is when I have the opportunity to summarize for the Judge the facts and law of the case and seek to influence how the Judge should rule, I first argued that Wendy was not competent to sign the amendment leaving all of the Trust property to Caregiver. And I argued that Caregiver unduly influenced Joe to sign the Amendment. Therefore Caregiver should receive nothing as a beneficiary of Joe's or Wendy's Trust. Then, as to Caregiver receiving the 50 percent of Joe's property in his survivor's Trust as an omitted spouse, I argued that Caregiver was NOT an omitted spouse because AFTER he married

> **The Judge asked me, "So what would Beth receive?" "Everything in Joe's estate," I answered. The Judge inquired, "And what is in Joe's estate?" "Nothing!" I replied, "as there is NOTHING in Joe's estate as EVERYTHING is in the Trust!" And that is exactly what the Judge ruled!**

Caregiver, Joe wrote a "testamentary" document (taking effect on his death), really a Will, leaving "my dog Puddypots and all of my estate to my wife, Caregiver." The Judge asked me, "So what would Caregiver receive?" "Everything in Joe's estate," I answered. The Judge inquired, "And what is in Joe's estate?" "NOTHING!" I exclaimed, "as there is NOTHING in Joe's estate because EVERYTHING is in the Trust!" And that is exactly what the Judge ruled!

About a week and a half after the trial, the Judge's decision arrived in the mail. The Amendment was not valid so Caregiver would receive nothing under the Trust document, and Beth would receive nothing as an omitted spouse because after his marriage to Beth, Joe signed a testamentary document leaving his entire estate to his spouse, Beth. Joe's estate had nothing, and the Trust had the house, which, the Trust provided, would go to my client. I don't think I had ever spoken with an angrier attorney, when Beth's attorney called me that afternoon.

Indeed, this was a tricky case, and it can be tricky to figure out how to avoid getting into such a predicament. In this case, Joe had no kids, but perhaps you can imagine the possibility that a caregiver could take advantage of your mother or father and even go so far as to marry your mother or father after one of them should pass. What a horrible nightmare! What we should not forget is that bad things CAN happen, not always to other people, but they can also happen to you! This possibility invites us to at least consider a rule that is so heartbreaking to even have to put into print.

CREATING YOUR ESTATE PLAN

What rule can you implement for your estate plan? How can you avoid this problem from arising with your family? After all, based on the Richard Pryor case, you may not be able to challenge one of your parent's marriage to their caregiver based on undue influence. And it doesn't appear that it would work to have your parent sign a statement in front of witnesses that any future marriage would be the product of fraud or undue influence unless the parent gave notice to one or more people. So, what can you do?

Certainly, it is important to choose your parents' caregivers wisely. Choose a reputable caregiver or caregiver company. Also, although not tested, it may be possible to prevent such wrongdoing on the part of a caregiver or other person unduly influencing your parent to marry them by basing a challenge to the marriage of your parent to their caregiver on a contract theory. That is, perhaps your parent can sign a contract with the beneficiaries of the Trust that in return for "assistance" (the consideration), the parent agrees not to get married, and thereby risk diluting the share of the Trust going to such beneficiaries, without 60-days written notice to the beneficiaries prior to the marriage. And perhaps further provide that any such future marriage not be subject to the probate code (state the code section) providing that such spouse would receive their spousal share.

It may also be a good idea to also have the caregiver sign a contract that they won't marry your mother or father. Until the California legislature amends the laws on this issue, a challenge to the marriage or the effects of marriage based on a contract, may be the only way to prevent such wrongdoing on the part of a caregiver or other person who unduly influences your mother or father to marry them. I think this Rule #11 is the most unusual rule in this guide. With the elderly living longer, and busy adult children commonly arranging for professional caregivers to assist in the care of their parents, this Rule #11 could quite possibly be one of the most important.

Recap of Rule #11: Have the caregiver sign a contract that as a condition of employment, he or she will not marry your mother or father.

Rule #12: If you use percentages or fractions in your Trust, make sure the math is correct.

People who place a very high importance on education might provide in their trust that their daughter would receive one-third of the Trust upon receiving a bachelor's degree, one-third upon receiving her master's degree, and one-third upon receiving her Ph.D. Although you may think in terms of 1/3, 1/3, and 1/3 fractions, the proper way to draft the provision is to have their daughter receiving <u>one-third (1/3)</u> upon receiving a bachelor's degree. Then <u>one-half (1/2)</u> of the balance would be distributed to their daughter upon her attaining a master's degree. And finally, the <u>100%</u> of the balance would be distributed upon their daughter attaining a Ph.D. Although this is written as "1/3, 1/2, 100%" language, the math really does accomplishes the parents' 1/3, 1/3, 1/3 goals. For example, if the Trust starts out with $100, then upon receiving a bachelor's degree, the daughter will receive one-third of $100, or $33.33, and there is $66.67 remaining. Then, assuming there is no growth of that $66.67, when the daughter receives her master's degree, the daughter will receive one-half of the balance of $66.67, or $33.33 again, leaving a remaining balance of $33.34 (adding a penny for rounding to the last distribution) . Finally, again assuming no growth of the $33.34 balance, upon receiving a Ph.D., the daughter will receive 100% of the balance, which is $33.34.

If a provision provided for distributions with language of 1/3, 1/3, and 1/3 rather than "1/3, 1/2, all," the first distribution would be $33.33, leaving a balance is $66.67. The second distribution would be 1/3 of $66.67, or $22.22, leaving a balance of $44.45. Finally, the third and final distribution would be 1/3 of $44.45, or $14.82, leaving a balance of $29.63 undistributed. There would still be a balance in the Trust when the parents intended that the entire Trust be distributed! Then there may need to be court involvement to determine the parents' true intent.

It is important to check your math whenever fractions or percentages are involved. My office settled a Trust that left various percentages to more than ten beneficiaries. But when I added up all of the percentages, they totaled only 99%. Who gets that remaining 1%? You may have seen various movies where the computer programmer designed a program to have all of the fractions of pennies diverted to his account. Well, an unscrupulous Trustee could pay everyone the percentages the Trust said to distribute and hope no one would notice the extra 1%. In this case the Trustee allocated the 1% pro rata, so that the beneficiaries getting a larger share of the total would get a larger portion of the remaining 1%. But who is to say that is the way to do it? A beneficiary who is getting a smaller share could challenge that method and argue that that extra 1% should be divided equally amongst the beneficiaries rather than pro-rata. In this case, no one complained, but someone could have. It is a good idea for the Trustee to get a signed consent from all beneficiaries prior to distributing so that the Trustee will know if any beneficiaries will complain or file a petition in court. If the numbers are big enough, there is a greater likelihood that someone will complain or file a petition. Therefore, it is important to be mindful of this next rule.

Recap of Rule #12: If you use percentages or fractions in your Trust, make sure the math is correct.

Rule #13: Rather than gifting your real estate to your kids during your lifetime or holding your real estate with your kids as joint tenants with right of survivorship, it is generally better to fund your real estate into your Trust and have your kids as the beneficiaries.

For the same reasons that parents add their children to their bank accounts, they also add the children to the title to their real property such as their house. Or they give their home outright to their adult children. There are a number of reasons this is not a good idea. One reason mentioned previously, is that the home will be at risk to creditors of the children. There is another important reason. That is that the children will lose the benefit of a step up in tax basis.

When a property is sold, the seller will have a gain on sale equal to the sales price less the tax basis. The tax basis is typically the purchase price, but may be adjusted upward for improvements and downward for prior depreciation that was allowed to be deducted perhaps because it was a rental or business property. Suppose parents purchased a house for $200,000 ten years ago, and now it is being sold for $320,000, and there are selling expenses of $20,000, including the realtor's commission. The gain is $320,000 less the basis of $200,000 less the selling expenses of $20,000, equaling a taxable gain of $100,000. Assuming federal and state taxes of 25%, the tax due on sale would be $25,000. However, since a married couple can exclude up to $500,000 of gain on the sale of their primary residence if they have lived in the home as their primary residence for two of the last five years, the parents would pay no tax on the $100,000 gain.

Suppose instead that the parents gifted their house to their son, and then their son sold the house. When there is a gift, there is a carryover of tax basis from the donor (the one giving the gift) to the donee (the one receiving the gift). The son would have the $200,000 basis, and have the same $100,000 taxable gain after the selling expenses. But the son didn't use the home as his primary residence so he would be stuck with paying the $25,000 in taxes.

Now suppose that the son received the house not by a gift from his parents, but rather by inheritance. If the parents owned the house when they died, the house would get a step up in basis equal to the fair market value. So if the son were to sell it immediately after inheriting it for $300,000, the basis would also be $300,000, and there would be no taxable gain and therefore no tax to pay!

What if the parents simply added their son as a co-owner during their lives? Well, if they added the son as a 50% co-owner, that is treated as a gift of 50%. The son would own 50% and the parents would own 50%. So when the parents pass, only half of the property would receive a step-up in basis to one-half of the $300,000, or $150,000. The son's basis would remain the one-half of the $200,000 original basis, or $100,000. After the parents' passing when the son inherits the other half of the house, the son's basis would be the $150,000 stepped-up basis on the 50% of the house he inherited, plus the son's $100,000 carryover basis on the 50% of the house his parents gifted to him, for a total of $250,000. If the son then sold the house for $320,000, after subtracting the basis of $250,000 and selling expenses of $20,000, the taxable gain would be $50,000, and the son would owe $12,500 in tax!

These examples illustrate that all else being equal, it is better to leave your real property to your children through your trust rather than give to your children or add them as a co-owner during your life.

Recap of Rule #13: Rather than gifting your real estate to your kids during your lifetime or holding your real estate with your kids as joint tenants with right of survivorship, it is generally better to fund your real estate into your Trust and have your kids as the beneficiaries.

Rule #14: Consider ways to pass your low property tax assessment to your heirs.

If you own a house or other real property, you are certainly aware of paying property taxes. Either you pay them through impounds with your mortgage payment or you pay them twice a year, by December 10 and April 10, or other such schedule your CPA may recommend. The amount of property tax is based on the assessed value, and in the old days in California, the Assessor could adjust the assessed value to the true market value each year. With property values increasing significantly in the 1970's, some homeowners were forced from their homes because they couldn't pay the property taxes. This changed in 1978 when California voters approved Proposition 13, which limited the annual tax increases to no more than 2%. Now, in California, the Assessor can increase the assessed value of a property by no more than 2% per year, unless, of course, there are improvements made to the property.

STEVE H. HORNSTEIN, ESQ., CPA, LL.M., CFP®

Homeowners love Prop. 13. The tax collector, the Assessor, hates it. People who have owned their property for a long time will generally find that their assessed value is significantly lower than the market value. So, the Assessor has been looking for ways to get rid of Prop. 13 or find a workaround in order to increase the assessed value to the market value, and thereby increase tax revenue. One way that the assessed value may be increased to the market value is the transfer of the property to a new owner. For example, if someone sells or even gives their property to another, the Assessor can reassess the property to the fair market value, typically the sales price. However, there is an exception to this ability of the Assessor to reassess the property. One such exception is Prop. 58, which allows an exclusion from reassessment if the property is transferred from a parent to a child. The term "child" doesn't mean that child is a minor (under 18); the child could be an adult. Another exception is Prop. 193, allowing the exclusion for transfers to grandchildren under certain circumstances. So all should be fine for parents wanting to leave property to their children and not have the property reassessed, yes?

Well, no, not all is fine. For people owning a home in their name or the name of their Trust, they could leave the property to their children and avoid reassessment. But most of the children would sell an inherited home anyway, as they may not want to move into it. However, parents with rental property may indeed want to pass their property to their children and not have it reassessed. It would be fine if they owned the rental property in their name or in the name of their Trust, but many people with rental property set up a business entity such as a Limited Liability Company ("LLC"). And this gives the Assessor a loophole to increase property taxes despite the exclusions of Prop. 58 and Prop. 193.

The Los Angeles County Assessor publishes a book called "Guide To Propositions 58 and 193." The guide says that "[T]ransfers of ownership interests in legal entities, aside from most trusts, do not qualify for the exclusion." The relevant provision from the guide is at #7, which states that "[T]ransfers of ownership interests in legal entities, aside from most trusts, *do not qualify for the exclusion.*" I have copied the excerpt below with my highlighting:

> 7. Transfers of ownership interests in legal entities, aside from most trusts, *do not qualify for the exclusion.*

Further, the "Assessors' Handbook, Section 401, Change in Ownership" published by the California State Board of Equalization, and last updated in September 2010, provides as follows:

PARENT-CHILD AND GRANDPARENT-
GRANDCHILD EXCLUSION

The parent-child and grandparent-grandchild exclusions apply only to transfers of real property; transfers of interests in legal entities that hold real property do not qualify. Thus, if property is held in a legal entity (for example, a family limited partnership), the property must first be transferred by the legal entity to the individual partners prior to the parent-child or grandparent-grandchild transfer in order to qualify for the exclusion. (See Chapter 7 for a discussion of the applicability of the step transaction doctrine to such transfers.

A lot of people hold rental property in LLC's or other entities, and many of them are counting on the parent to child exclusion from reassessment. I expect a lot of people will be surprised that their kids won't get the exclusion. So, I am getting the word out.

I brought it to the attention at a meeting of attorneys at the end of 2013. Indeed, many did not know that if their clients' real property is in an LLC or other such legal entity, they won't get the exclusion and their property will be reassessed even if they leave their LLC to their kids. Note that the Guide indicates that it was published in 2010, and three years later, many attorneys still don't know about it. The Assessor does not make a big effort to inform the public of its loophole to deny people the Prop. 58 parent to child exclusion from an increase in property taxes. The Assessor sends that booklet with its letter denying the exclusion, by which time it is too late to do anything about it. This loophole allowing the Assessor to deny Prop. 58 exclusions will certainly become known to more and more families over time, but I would like to help people learn about it in advance so that they are not surprised when it is too late to do anything about it.

For those people facing this problem, but still desiring the protections of an LLC, it is important to consult with an attorney knowledgeable in this area, or their family will face unnecessarily high property taxes later. My office assists families in developing strategies and methods of holding real estate to help prevent the loss of the exclusion (and make sure that significant income tax benefits, such as the ability to have a step up in tax basis, discussed in Rule #13, are preserved too). After all, if the assessed value were to go up by $800,000, the property taxes may go up by at least $10,000. But remember that property taxes are due every year, and considering the possible 2% increases on top of that, the additional cost would likely be over $100,000 over ten years, making Rule #14 extremely important to those families desiring to leave property to their children.

Recap of Rule #14: Consider ways to pass your low property tax assessment to your heirs.

Rule #15: Make sure that your agent appointed in your Advance Health Care Directive has the power to receive information from your doctor if your Durable Power of Attorney for Financial Affairs requires that a doctor must determine that you are not competent before it becomes effective.

A power of attorney (POA) is a document in which the "principal," the person creating the document, appoints someone, their "agent" to act on their behalf in order to handle the affairs for them, such as writing checks to pay bills or speak with the principal's insurance company to handle issues on behalf of the principal, or do other things on behalf of the principal. The principal may make the POA a "general" POA or a "durable" POA (DPA). A general POA allows the agent to do only what the principal could do. So, if the principal were to become incapacitated, the agent would not be able to do anything because the principal can't do anything. On the other hand, the agent's powers under a durable POA continue beyond the principal's incapacity so that the agent can continue to perform the powers specified in the document. Generally, all of the POAs we prepare in my office are durable rather than general POAs. After all, the reason that most people want a POA in the first place is to allow someone to take care of things if they become unable to do so. For example, consider the problems that could arise for Joe and his family if either of these scenarios were to happen: 1) If Joe were in a car accident and had to stay in the hospital for a few weeks, and therefore unable to write checks for a few weeks, or 2) If Joe were to get Alzheimers and become permanently unable to write checks. If Joe had a durable POA (DPA), his agent under his would then be able to take Joe's DPA to the bank to become a signer on his account so that the agent can write checks on Joe's account to pay important bills such as his rent or mortgage payment, or the electric, gas and water bills.

Under a general power of attorney, Joe's agent would be unable to write checks if Joe can't write checks. So for estate planning purposes, it is important that the POA be "durable" rather than "general." In fact, the agent could even handle putting assets into the principal's Trust, such assets as the bank account itself, or perhaps the principal's house that may have been inadvertently left out of Trust. Remember, should the principal pass away, all powers of attorney become inoperable, be they general POAs (effective when the principal is competent) or durable POAs (effective even when the principal is incompetent). No POAs are operable when the principal is deceased. At that time we would be looking to the principal's Trust for assets funded into the Trust, or the principal's Will for assets outside of the principal's Trust which may require a probate to administer.

Once we determine that a durable POA (DPA) is appropriate, the next issue is to determine whether to make the DPA effective immediately or "springing." If the DPA is "springing," it will become effective only when the principal becomes incapacitated. Then the issue is who makes that determination that the principal is incapacitated. Often, attorneys will write into the DPAs that the determination is to be made by two doctors. That can be a hassle because then the agent has to take the principal to two doctors to get letters to attach to the DPA to show the banks or whoever else needs to confirm that the DPA is effective. This task can become even more difficult if the principal under the DPA is not the named agent in the principal's health care directive. Then, that agent under the health care directive will have to get the letters from the doctors.

But, what if the health care directive becomes effective only on the incapacity of the principal? In such a case, the first doctor would be unable to release the principal's health information as it is not effective unless there are two doctors certifying that the principal is not competent. But that doctor is just one doctor. Unless another doctor also so certifies, the principal will not be deemed incapacitated for purposes of the health care directive being effective. Thus, the doctor can't release the doctor's certification to the agent under the health care directive saying that the principal is incapacitated, and thus the DPA will likewise not be able to become effective. We have a catch 22 in which the DPA and health care directive aren't effective until two doctors certify that the principal is incapacitated. But the doctors can't release the certifications until two doctors give the certifications to the agent under the health care directive, which they can't do until the health care directive becomes effective, which they can't do until two doctors certify…, and so on and so on. You can see that poorly drafted documents can turn an already difficult situation into a real nightmare.

We typically have all of our DPAs for financial matters and health care directives effective immediately so that there is no need to take the principal to the doctor to get the certifications of incapacity. On the unusual occasion that the DPA is springing, we certainly have the health care directive effective immediately so that the agent has the ability to get needed medical records and certifications of incapacity from the principals's doctors. This rule is very important to ensure the estate plan can be put into action when it is needed!

Recap of Rule #15: Make sure that your agent appointed in your Advance Health Care Directive has the power to receive information from your doctor if your Durable Power of Attorney for Financial Affairs requires that a doctor must determine that you are not competent before it becomes effective.

Rule #16: Make sure that you don't sabotage the plan that your adult children have for their children (your grandchildren).

If you have adult children, especially if they have kids, you should talk to them about getting their estate plan in order. After all, they've got your grandchildren to protect! Speaking of grandchildren, it is important to think not only down one generation, but perhaps down another generation or more to make sure that you don't subvert the plan that your children have for their children (your grandkids). For example, your daughter and her husband may provide in their Trust that their children get their distribution upon them reaching age 25 if they have attained a degree from a four year accredited university but if they didn't, then they must wait until they are age 30. If you simply give their children money from your Trust upon them reaching age 21, then you will have made your daughter's and her husband's Trust less effective or possibly completely ineffective in carrying out their intentions. It is important that your Trust is "in sync" with that of your daughters' Trust or estate plan.

If your estate plan provides that if your child predeceases distribution, that the Trust's assets goes to your child's children (your grandkids) outright at age 21, but your child's (adult child) Trust provides that his or her children (your grandkids) get the distribution outright at age 25 if they have graduated from college, but age 30 if they haven't graduated from college, then you have just sabotaged your adult child's estate plan. After all, your grandchildren don't have to worry about having to graduate from college to get a distribution from their parents' Trust because they get a distribution from their grandparent's Trust (your Trust) at age 21. So, despite your adult child's efforts to encourage their children (your grandchildren) to go to college by delaying distribution until after they graduate from college, your estate plan leaving your grandchildren a distribution outright at age 21 without regard to whether they have graduated from college undermines your adult child's plan for their children (your grandchildren).

> **"You can make sure your estate plan does not sabotage the plan that your adult children have for their children (your grandchildren) by making sure that your estate plan is "in sync" with your children's estate plans."**

You can make sure your estate plan does not sabotage the plan that your adult children have for their children (your grandchildren) by making sure that your estate plan is "in sync" with your children's estate plans. Therefore, while you are preparing your estate plan and thinking about provisions relating to your grandchildren, it is often a good idea to consult with your adult children about what they have in their estate plan, or if they don't have one, then find out what they would like to include in their estate plan when they get one. If they haven't given it any thought, then perhaps you can get the discussion started. Don't let your adult child's lack of an estate plan delay you from getting yours, for without an estate plan, the distribution age is 18, which is younger than most people would like their kids and grandkids to get a large sum of money outright. When your adult child finally gets around to doing his or her estate plan, you can amend your Trust to be in sync with your adult child's estate plan.

If you disagree with your children's estate plan, you can, of course, sabotage their plan if you so desire. For example, if your adult child's estate plan has his or her children (your grandchildren) having to wait until they are 40 years old to receive their distribution outright, and you think they should receive their distribution at age 25, you certainly can have your estate plan distribute to your grandchildren at age 25. But if you would rather not sabotage your children's estate plan, then remember this Rule #16.

Recap of Rule #16: Make sure that you don't sabotage the plan that your children have for their children (your grandchildren).

Rule #17: If you are married, make sure you choose the right type of "married person" trust to make.

When a married couple set up a trust, there are typically four types of married person trusts from which to choose:

1. Marital Trust

2. AB Trust

3. Marital Disclaimer Trust

4. ABC Trust

The type of trust chosen has important ramifications to the creators of the trust. Below is an explanation of each type of Trust that a married couple may choose.

Marital Trust

With a "marital trust" when one spouse dies, the surviving spouse has complete control over all of the trust property, unless some property is to be distributed upon the passing of the first spouse to pass (the "deceased spouse"). That is, the surviving spouse can:

1. Change the beneficiaries of the trust; and

2. Use all Trust property during his or her life; and

3. Spend all of the money in the trust.

AB Trust

To better understand this type of Trust, a brief background will be helpful. This explanation will get a little technical, but only to the extent of what is needed for a reasonable explanation of an AB Trust. An AB Trust became popular as a tool for reducing or eliminating estate taxes. An "estate tax" has been imposed on large estates for many years. When someone dies, if the net value of their estate, or the value after deducting debts, exceeds a specified exemption, that estate will be subject to a tax at rates that over the years has generally been in the range of 35% to 55%. The exemption has risen over the years. In 1997, the exemption was $600,000. Under the American Taxpayer Relief Act of 2012 (ATRA), the exemption was raised to $5 million (this amount adjusts annually for inflation). Congress could change this exemption amount in the future.

Just for illustration purposes, let's assume the exemption is $1 million. Suppose that Husband and Wife have an estate with a net value of $2 million, and all of their property is "community property," which means property acquired during marriage. Let's assume they have no "separate property," which is property acquired prior to marriage. Suppose Husband dies first. If they had a marital trust, the entire trust estate would go to the wife and she would have total control over it. So, that means that Wife's estate would now be $2 million. Suppose she then dies a week after Husband. Since her estate is over the $1 million exemption by the amount of $1 million ($2 million estate less $1 million exemption = $1 million subject to tax).

Her estate would be subject to the estate tax on the $1 million. If the tax rate were 45%, that would mean a tax of $450,000.

An AB Trust was a simple way for a husband and a wife to avoid this estate tax, by not wasting the Husband's $1 million exemption. See, in the above example, all of the property went to the Wife, without using any of Husband's exemption. If Husband and Wife had an AB Trust, then when Husband dies, the Trust is split into an "A" Trust, also called the "survivor's Trust" and a "B" Trust, also called the "Bypass Trust" because it "bypasses" the estate of the surviving spouse. The B Trust is an irrevocable Trust. That is, the surviving spouse cannot change it. Wife's portion of the Trust would go into her "A" Trust, which is treated just like the marital trust. Wife has complete control over the A Trust. Husband's half of the community property goes into his "B" Trust. Note that if Husband had separate property, that property would also go to the B Trust. The maximum amount going to the B Trust cannot exceed the estate tax exemption. Wife does not have total control over the B Trust. While Wife gets the income of the B Trust for her lifetime, and she gets the principal for her health, education, maintenance, and support (although we generally provide that she cannot get the principal until she has spent all of her A Trust), she cannot change the beneficiaries of the B Trust. Since Wife cannot change the beneficiaries of the B Trust, that means that the Trust is not treated as being in her estate, but rather is treated as being part of Husband's estate. That means that the $1 million in the B Trust is protected by his $1 million exemption! So, if Wife were to die a week after Husband, she only has in her estate the $1 million in her A Trust, and since the estate exemption is $1 million, none of her estate is subject to the estate tax. Furthermore, since all of the B Trust is exempted from estate tax, in the unlikely event that the B Trust were to grow to $10 million in that week, there is still no estate tax to pay when the Trust distributes to the beneficiaries upon the death of Wife.

After the American Taxpayer Relief Act of 2012 (ATRA), there was not as much of a need for an AB Trust for estate tax savings because ATRA allows a carry of unused exemption to the surviving spouse. Also, with the exemption growing to over $5 million per spouse (now over $11 million beginning in 2018), not as many people were affected by estate tax. Nevertheless, there is another important reason to have an AB Trust even for smaller estates.

Remember that with a Marital Trust, the surviving spouse has complete control over the Trust and can change the beneficiaries. Suppose that Husband and Wife each has a child from a prior marriage, and suppose their Trust leaves their property 50% to Husband's child and 50% to Wife's child. Now suppose that Husband dies first. Wife would be able to disinherit Husband's child! On the other hand, if they had an AB Trust, and all of their property were community property, one-half of the property would go to the A Trust and the other half to the B Trust. Now, Wife can only change the beneficiaries of her one-half of the property in the A Trust. She cannot change the beneficiaries of the B Trust! The B Trust would remain with the

STEVE H. HORNSTEIN, ESQ., CPA, LL.M., CFP®

beneficiaries being 50% to Husband's child and 50% to Wife's child, even if Wife changed the beneficiary of her A Trust to be only her child. When there are children from prior marriages, it is important to consider an AB Trust as an alternative to a Marital Trust to prevent the possibility of the children of the deceased spouse from being disinherited.

An AB Trust can also limit a wrongdoer's ability to commit a fraud upon your family. We have seen several situations where people take advantage of the elderly after their spouse passes away. For example, a wrongdoer influenced a man after his wife passed away to change the family Trust to leave all of his property to the wrongdoer. Since the man and deceased wife had an AB Trust, the wife's portion of the Trust became irrevocable when she died. Therefore the surviving husband only had the power to change his half. So, even if a wrongdoer were successful in perpetrating such a fraud, his ill-gained bounty would be cut by half if the Trust were an AB Trust.

There are a few downsides to an AB Trust. For example, if there were a good reason for the surviving spouse to alter the distribution of the B Trust, such as perhaps the child developed a drug problem that would make it a good idea to delay the age at which the child would receive a distribution, the surviving spouse could not do so. The surviving spouse would only be able to alter the surviving spouse's portion of the Trust (the A Trust), not the decedent's portion that became irrevocable upon his or her passing (the B Trust). Also, the B Trust has additional costs of ongoing administration, such as preparing a separate tax return each year.

There are benefits as well as costs associated with an AB Trust. It is important to consider the family situation in determining whether an AB Trust is appropriate. Depending on the family situation, the benefits of an AB Trust could far outweigh the costs.

Marital Disclaimer Trust

A Marital Disclaimer Trust is the type of Trust most commonly chosen by our clients that do not have children through prior marriages or when the family situation indicates that the surviving spouse treats the spouse's children as his or her own. With a Marital Disclaimer Trust, the trust is treated like a Marital Trust. That is, the spouse would have complete control over the entire trust. However, the surviving spouse is given the option to "disclaim" property. That is, the surviving spouse can choose to not accept a portion or all of the deceased spouse's share of property, and that disclaimed property would go to the deceased spouse's B Trust. The B Trust is only set up if the surviving spouse disclaims property. This way, the Trust can operate as a Marital Trust, but if it turns out that an AB Trust would have been beneficial, the Trust can be made to operate as a B Trust. If Congress changed the law to not allow a carryover of the deceased spouse's unused estate tax exemption to the surviving spouse, an AB Trust would be beneficial because it would allow the deceased spouse's estate tax exemption to be preserved. A Marital Disclaimer gives the surviving spouse options to assess what the situation is when the time comes and make a decision as to whether to have the Trust operate as a Marital Trust or an AB Trust.

ABC Trust

An ABC Trust is rarer in our practice as it comes in to play for much larger estates. Using the prior example, suppose that Husband and Wife have an estate of $3 million rather than $2 million. Now Husband's share is $1.5 million. Assuming that the exemption is $1 million, only $1 million can go to Husband's B Trust. As for Husband's remaining $500,000 share of community property, if Husband and Wife had an AB Trust, then that remaining $500,000 would go to the Marital Trust and the surviving spouse would have complete control over it. On the other hand, if the trust were an ABC Trust, then the remaining $500,000 would go to a "C "Trust. This C Trust is treated as an irrevocable trust as is the B Trust. That means that the surviving spouse cannot make any changes to it. However, the surviving spouse still gets the income from it and can get the principal for his or her health, education, maintenance, and support. However, unlike the B Trust that is treated as not being in the estate of the surviving spouse, the C Trust is treated as being in the estate of the surviving spouse, and therefore subject to estate tax if the surviving spouse's estate exceeds the estate tax exemption upon the death of the surviving spouse. A reason for choosing an ABC Trust would be to have Husband's portion of the community property that exceeds the amount that can go to the B Trust go to the C Trust so that it still goes to a Trust that is irrevocable and can't be changed by the surviving spouse. An ABC Trust may require an additional fee.

Here is a simple summary of these four types of trusts that a married couple may choose:

1. If you wish to keep it the simplest, you may wish to choose to have a <u>Marital Trust</u>, in which the surviving spouse has full control over the Trust assets.

2. You may wish to choose an <u>AB Trust</u> if you have a child from a prior marriage or otherwise desire to have all or a portion of your separate property or your share of community property held in an irrevocable trust with your spouse being unable to make changes to it.

3. The most commonly chosen type of Trust for married individuals is a <u>Marital Disclaimer Trust</u>, which gives the surviving spouse to choose at the time of the death of the first spouse whether to treat the Trust as a Marital Trust or an AB Trust.

4. If you have a large estate and are concerned about Congress one day getting rid of the carryover of unused exemption to a spouse, then you may wish to choose an <u>ABC Trust</u>.

If you need further assistance in choosing the type of Trust that is right for you, you should speak with your attorney.

Recap of Rule #17: If you are married, make sure you choose the right type of "married person" trust to make.

Rule #18: Look at problems in the relationships of your family members as they exist today, so that you can reasonably anticipate the problems that are likely to exist in the future, and take steps to prevent these future problems.

You may be thinking that the issue of who might not be happy with your estate plan is irrelevant. After all, it is your plan, so it's no one else's business. If someone doesn't like it, and for anyone other than you - too bad; deal with it. The problem with this position is that if someone is unhappy, they might challenge your plan. And you won't be there to defend it so your heirs and beneficiaries may be spending the money you left for your family on legal bills that could go on for years.

You may be able to avoid this unnecessary cost by anticipating future problems. An experienced attorney should be able to help you to foresee what may happen in the future because the attorney has likely seen many family situations that ended up in litigation and can help you to foresee issues that could arise with your family. For example, if you wish to leave more to one child than another, and the child getting less is expecting to receive the same as his or her sibling, the emotional character of that sibling should be discussed. How might that sibling react to receiving less? Is he likely to seek an attorney to challenge your Trust? If so, steps can be taken now to prevent that. Or, perhaps you should include language in your Trust to make a challenge less likely to succeed or even be attempted.

Be especially cautious if you have been diagnosed with Alzheimer's disease, even if it is in its very early stages. Consider that someone may use that diagnosis as a weapon to challenge your Trust or your amendments to your Trust that are signed after your diagnosis. I have seen children challenge an amendment of a couple married for 37 years based on the mother being diagnosed with Alzheimer's. The husband in this case was a stepfather to the children. Despite being married to their mother for 37 years, the children accused their stepfather of unduly influencing their mother to allow her husband to live in the house for the remainder of his life if she should die before her husband. There are precautions that can be taken to prevent such a challenge to your estate plan if you have an infirmity such as Alzheimer's that others could use to challenge your estate plan. You could get a certificate of independent review at the time of signing. You could get a checkup by your doctor and have a mental status examination and document the results. You can also speak about your wishes for your estate plan to a number of people and document with whom you spoke. These people may be witnesses at a future trial to thwart your estate plan from being undone by a Judge.

Even if you don't have an infirmity such as Alzheimer's, bc especially cautious if you or your spouse have stepchildren. I am not talking about children that you adopted and treat as your own children along with your children from your own blood. I am talking about children who are the children of your spouse but not of you. My office handled particularly bitter litigation between stepbrothers and sisters whose parents had passed away. The litigation started when the husband died and his four adult children went to the house with a U-Haul truck to take all of what they considered his belongings, while his wife was still residing in the home! The wife, and mother to three children of her own could have been considered to be not of sound mind, especially immediately after her husband had passed away. At the very least, she could be said to be easily susceptible to undue influence, and the father's four kids claimed that his surviving spouse had given them the property that they took away with a U-Haul truck. The father's four kids took a vast gun collection, cars, and allegedly $40,000 in cash as well as, incidentally to the main issues, the father's social security check that just happened to be cashed by a son bearing the same name as the father, only with a "Jr." at the end of it. The husband had expensive hobbies and spent a lot of money on accumulating collections of guns, coins, and various other items that had fairly substantial value. The wife did not spend money on collectibles. Although the husband and wife had written their Trust to split all of their property evenly among their 7 children and step-children, the husband's four children thought that they should get their father's various collections. So they did what four adult children do when they think they should have things. They drove a U-Haul truck over and took them!

The mother's three adult kids sued the father's four adult kids for the return of trust property. The mother died several months later. If you don't think estate planning litigation is among the most contentious of all matters, think again. There was simply not enough money or assets at stake to justify what the litigation appeared would cost. So the parties agreed to try mediation, which is a meeting in front of a mediator who first meets with everyone together, and then moves the parties to separate rooms to meet with each side separately. Often mediators attempt to simply see if there is a middle ground at which the parties can reach a settlement, running back and forth between the rooms with offers until a deal is reached. This mediator worked differently. This mediator, a retired judge, meets with both sides and then comes up with a settlement that he thinks should be agreed to by all.

We started at 10AM on Tuesday morning. The first three hours, at $500 per hour, were used by the mediator to explain the process and how he works, do a conflict of interest check to see if there was any reason he couldn't handle our case, and get other formalities out of the way. This mediator took pride in having mediated 896 prior cases, including a $40 million suit involving one of the big oil companies, which the mediator appeared proud to say had been his longest mediation to date at seventeen straight hours! He saw the look of horror on my face at learning this as we had to return to court in our case the next day at 8:30AM. The mediator reassured me that a mediation lasting seventeen hours was very unusual, and, after all, that was a large and complicated multi-million dollar suit involving a big oil company. Well, eighteen hours later, at around 4am the next morning, I noticed we had broken the record. But we weren't done yet.

With venomous emotions between the step-kids that had built up over the years now coming to a climax among the exhausted litigants, everyone desired to finally bring this case to an end and avoid the added costs of a trial. So everyone went along with the retired judge's suggested settlement. Twenty hours and $10,000 of mediation fees later, we were out of there. However, the judge's suggested settlement included both sides returning to him in case of any unresolved issues, and in the half hour we had to draft the settlement agreement, the agreement left openings for further dispute. We had to return to this judge again for binding arbitration. A little over two years after that, the assets of the trust were distributed and the case was done.

And a big lesson was learned. The lesson to be learned here is that we should all anticipate that when we see distrust and disputes among family members during our lives, perhaps our children and stepchildren, we should not expect these problems to end when we are no longer here, or able, to handle them. Such disputes may likely continue after you are gone. For this family, had the husband and wife properly recognized and anticipated the problems that would likely continue after they were gone, steps could have been taken to add language to their

> "The lesson to be learned here is that we should all anticipate that when we see distrust and disputes among family members during our lives, perhaps our children and stepchildren, we should not expect these problems to end when we are no longer here, or able, to handle them."

Trust to make clear their intentions regarding the distribution of personal property that each of them owned. By addressing, within the Trust document, the specific beneficiaries and the timing of distributions, that is, who would be the specific beneficiaries of various items of personal property and whether such distributions would be made upon the passing of one or both of the spouses, the litigation among family members could have been avoided. This rule is one of the cornerstones of a successful estate plan. An experienced attorney who has seen many issues arise in the past can be of great help to you in addressing this Rule #18.

Recap of Rule #18: Look at problems in the relationships of your family members as they exist today, so that you can reasonably anticipate the problems that are likely to exist in the future, and take steps to prevent these future problems.

HONORABLE MENTIONS

Here are some rules that didn't make the top 18, but are still important:

1. **Don't count on having one beneficiary paying the other beneficiaries to buy out the other beneficiaries' share of a property.** It is extremely rare that they will agree on a purchase price! Consider a mother who left her estate equally to her three children and one of the children wants to keep her house and buy out his siblings' 2/3 interest in

the house. The son who wants the property will benefit from a low valuation that reduces how much he has to pay his siblings, while the other beneficiaries will benefit from a high valuation that increases the purchase price of each of their 1/3 interest in the property. They may get their own appraisers but if the appraisals aren't exactly the same number, they may argue about the purchase price. Often, the only to ensure that the purchase price is fair is to list the house for sale and have the beneficiary who wants it bid on the house with the rest of the world. Then if the son is the highest bidder, there is no way anyone can say the son took advantage of the other beneficiaries, his siblings, and got too good of a deal.

2. Consider the role that a child's spouse may play. Your child may be just fine with your estate plan, but his or her spouse may not be. Sometimes we have seen that the spouse of the child is the one making the decisions, and despite your discussions with your child as to how things should be, his or her spouse has different ideas. Sometimes the discretion that the parent thought their child would be exercising is really being exercised by that child's spouse, whose ideas of how things should be are very different from the child, and what the parent discussed with the child. This is important to consider when choosing to have such a child as Trustee, as the parent may really be appointing that child's spouse as defacto Trustee.

3. Choose your battles wisely! This rule is generally for the

beneficiaries to consider after the Settlor passes away, but often, this rule is for everyone to consider in all aspects of their life. People often have complaints about all sorts of things. Maybe you were left 40% of the Trust while your sibling got 60%, and you are bitter that you didn't get an equal portion. If the net estate were $200,000, then the difference between your 40% and the 50% you think you should have gotten is 10% or $20,000. Give great thought as to whether it is worth petitioning the court, and all of the stress that entails, for $20,000. Some battles are worth fighting, and some are not. Sometimes people want to fight based on "Principal," arguing, "That's just not right no matter how much money is involved." Well, things may not be right, in your opinion, but there are a lot of other things in the world, and maybe other things in your life too that aren't right either. Perhaps part of the satisfaction in pursuing the litigation is more about harming the other beneficiary rather than benefiting yourself. Well, consider if that is really the best use of your resources. Perhaps your money and time may better be spent on other issues. The billionaire investor George Soros realized that there were issues in the world that needed fixing. Of course, you can fix a lot with a billion dollars. But George Soros made his billion go further by analyzing where his money and his time could make the biggest difference, and that's where he allocated his money and time. I think all of us can learn from this philosophy.

PART 3: HAVING AN ESTATE PLAN PREPARED BY AN ATTORNEY WITH PROFESSIONAL CONSULTATION COMPARED WITH A "DO-IT-YOURSELF" ESTATE PLAN — WHICH TYPE OF PREPARATION IS RIGHT FOR YOU?

There are several options available for you to get an estate plan prepared, and the differences in price are vast. You could spend a few hundred dollars for a "Do-It-Yourself" estate plan without an attorney, or you could go to an attorney and have one professionally prepared for a range of prices from $1,000 to $5,000 or more for a comprehensive plan to over $100,000 if more complicated tax planning is involved. You could get a "Do-It-Yourself" plan by going online and filling out a questionnaire and having an estate plan automatically prepared for you, or you could get "Do-It-Yourself" forms with blanks to fill in. Certainly, the more complicated your issues and the larger your estate, the greater the likelihood that you need to hire an experienced attorney to guide you through your complicated issues and help ensure that your issues are addressed appropriately. But what if you don't have a large estate, is one of those "Do-It-Yourself" plans ok for these people? Maybe it is; or maybe it isn't. That's the risk you take. I am a "Do-It-Yourselfer" in many areas of my life. When the plastic blinds covering the windows break off, I cut a piece of thick paper off of a cereal box, fold it over and scotch tape it to the broken part of the blind and Presto, it's like new! When the toilet handle breaks, I often have great success fixing it with a paperclip. Of course, when these "Do-It-Myself" fixes don't last, I can get more silly putty, chewing gum, paper clips, and cereal boxes, and make it all like new again. When it still doesn't last, as a last resort, I can call a professional to do it right!

There are two big things to keep in mind. In all of my "Do-It-Myself" projects, I have the opportunity to call a professional to get things done right if my paperclip or double stick tape doesn't work. That isn't the case with estate planning. When someone passes away, or even when the person becomes incapacitated, it is generally too late to fix things that were done wrong. The second big thing to keep in mind is that I limit my "Do-It-Myself" projects to things that aren't so important if there are problems. If the blind falls off my window again, it's not a big deal. But what about replacing an entire window and wanting assurance that it is secured properly and won't fall on someone? For that I would hire a professional. While I might use a paperclip to fix a toilet handle, would I attempt to replace the main water pipe from the street to my house? Flooding the neighborhood is not a risk I am willing to take, so I would call a professional plumber. Similarly, I view estate planning as one of those big things. If there is a problem in handling the entirety of my estate, all of my and my wife's assets, protecting and providing security for my family, my children, and my pets, that's a big deal and not something I would leave to a "Do-It-Myself" project if I weren't particularly trained in estate planning.

In Part 2 of this guide, I discuss eighteen rules covering issues and problems I have encountered in my estate planning law practice. But these eighteen rules don't cover every issue that could arise. How many issues have been litigated in probate court? Probably thousands. A skilled attorney can assist you in identifying the issues that are important to you and your family and help avoid problems from arising in the future.

> **"I recognize that there are many people who would not get an estate plan at all if it meant spending more than they could afford on an attorney. Indeed, a lower cost "Do-It-Yourself" plan may be fine to address their issues, especially if the alternative was to have no plan at all."**

Those people desiring more assurance that their estate plan will protect themselves and their families appropriately, an estate plan prepared in consultation with an attorney certainly provides more assurance than a "Do-It-Yourself" plan. But I recognize that there are many people who would not get an estate plan at all if it meant spending more than they could afford on an attorney. Indeed, a lower cost "Do-It-Yourself" plan may be fine to address their issues, especially if the alternative was to have no plan at all. But these estate planning "Do-It-Yourselfers" should, if possible, educate themselves as best they can, and the best place to start is by reading this guide.

I don't take the position that a "Do-It-Yourself" estate plan is a bad thing. For some people, it may be very appropriate. I just think that many people need to be more educated before they take the "Do-It-Yourself" route. Many people who purchased "Do-It-Yourself" estate plans may have no idea that important issues may not be addressed in their plans, and once they pass away, it is most likely too late to fix the problems. Likewise, some people who purchase a costly plan with detailed consultation with an attorney may have no idea that an inexpensive "Do-It-Yourself" estate plan would have worked fine for them. However, for these people, the added assurance of having the estate plan professionally prepared by an attorney is often worth the cost.

> "I don't take the position that a "Do-It-Yourself" estate plan is a bad thing. For some people, it may be very appropriate. I just think that many people need to be more educated before they take the "Do-It-Yourself" route."

Many people have come to my office to review their Trust or help settle their parents' estate and Trust. My office has often found problems with estate plans whether or not the plan was prepared in a "Do-It-Yourself" manner or was prepared in consultation with an attorney. However, as should be expected, we find more problems, both in terms of number as well as severity, with the "Do-It-Yourself" plans. For example, we have found problems with the Funding (see Rule #8). Many times, the Trust is not funded at all, which means that the Trust does not govern anything, and won't govern anything until the Will is administered, which may require an expensive probate). And sometimes in that instance we have found that the Will does not have the Trust as a beneficiary, which means that no property would <u>ever</u> get to the Trust, which means that the Trust would <u>never</u> govern anything.

This is not to say that problems can't arise with documents prepared by an attorney. I have reviewed Trusts, both "Do-It-Yourself" Trusts and Trusts prepared by an attorney that forgot to name any beneficiaries at all! However, again, it is important to note that I do find, by a very large margin, less problems with attorney prepared documents than I find with "Do-It-Yourself" documents. Attorney consultation is often very important. After all, if my clients who had the Trust with no named beneficiaries had not had me or my office review their documents, they may never have known that their estate plan had no named beneficiaries. At least, for these people who came to my office for a review, there was time to fix it, for once the creators of the documents (Settlors) pass away, it is most likely too late to fix the documents and either the family suffers the consequences of terrible documents, or they suffer the costs of going to court to attempt to straighten things out.

What should you do? Should you have an attorney prepared estate plan or a "Do-It-Yourself" estate plan? Generally, if you are well read in the estate planning area, and if your net estate will be less than the amount at which estate tax will be an issue, and if you and your spouse have no children that are not children of both of you, and if you understand all of the rules in this guide and none of the rules raise any red flags for you, and if you would not get an estate plan at all if you had to incur the higher cost of an attorney prepared plan, then for you and your family, a "Do-It-Yourself" estate plan may be the way to go. On the other hand, if you understand the importance of having high quality documents oversee the entirety of everything you have accumulated over your entire life, and you think the added assurance of attorney consultation is worth the relatively small additional cost, then professionally prepared documents may be a benefit to you and your family. Obviously, I am biased in favor of attorney prepared documents, not because I want to create full employment for attorneys. On the contrary, the more poorly drafted documents there are today, the more litigation and court hearings and mediations and other work there will be for attorneys tomorrow.

> "Obviously, I am biased in favor of attorney prepared documents, not because I want to create full employment for attorneys. On the contrary, the more poorly drafted documents there are today, the more work there will be for attorneys tomorrow."

Whichever type of preparation you choose, attorney prepared or "Do-It-Yourself" prepared, you can get either type through

Hornstein Law Offices. If you are still uncertain which type of preparation is appropriate for you, filling out a Trust questionnaire at www.HornsteinTrust.com is a great place to start. You can start filling out your questionnaire online and after you have completed your questionnaire, you can have a complimentary review with the staff at Hornstein Law Offices to assess if you think it would be a good idea to pursue further consultation with an attorney. At that time, you can choose whether to have your "Do-It-Yourself" <u>Basic Trust Package</u> prepared with the information you provided on your questionnaire, or whether you wish to have attorney consultation and have a <u>Comprehensive Trust Package</u> prepared.

In Part 4 of this guide, you will find out detailed information on how to get started in getting your own estate plan, regardless of whether you choose a "Do-It-Yourself" plan or an estate plan professionally prepared by an attorney. Whichever plan you choose, whether the Basic Trust Package (the "Do-It-Yourself" package) or the Comprehensive Trust Package, you can rest assured that the Trust will be of high quality. The "Do-It-Yourself" Basic Trust Package is of higher quality than other "Do-It-Yourself" plans. The "Do-It-Yourself" plan is still prepared by a law firm, Hornstein Law Offices, a multi-year winner of the Daily News Reader's Choice Award for "Best Living Trust." In order to keep down the cost of the "Do-It-Yourself" package, it omits some features that are included in the Comprehensive Trust Package, which includes attorney consultation. Should you choose to have a Comprehensive Trust Package prepared, you will be getting the highest quality

Trust package available anywhere. On the following pages is a chart comparing the two packages. Of course, fees and packages may change from time to time, so please see the most current chart at www.HornsteinTrust.com.

Comparison of Hornstein Trust Packages

	Comprehensive Trust Package	Basic Trust Package (Do-It-Yourself package)
Cost/ Minimum Fee	INDIVIDUAL: $2,250 MARRIED OR JOINT: $2,850 (Legal consultation, explanation, and document review, and assistance with choosing the appropriate type of Trust, and assistance with funding your Trust, and detailed document drafting specific to your circumstances. Note that unusual issues may require an additional fee.)	INDIVIDUAL: $795 MARRIED/ JOINT: $995 (Legal consultation and assistance and time drafting specific language are not included.)

	Comprehensive Trust Package	Basic Trust Package (Do-It-Yourself package)
Documents included	A Trust Book containing a Living Trust, which will be either a Single person Trust, or if you are married, a Marital Trust, A-B Trust, A-B-C Trust, or a Marital-Disclaimer Trust (we will analyze your situation and discuss with you to help you choose the appropriate type of trust); Trustee Instructions; Successor Trustee Instructions; Guidelines for the Successor Trustee; Funding documents including a Declaration of Intent and Assignment of Assets and up to two California deeds and a title search to determine the current title and property description per the last vesting deeds (states other than California and nontraditional properties such as timeshares require additional cost); Pour-over Will(s); Durable Power(s) of Attorney for Management of Property and Financial Affairs; Advance Health Care Directive(s); Physician's Directives; Anatomical Gift Form(s); a Location Key Guide (to help you in cataloging all of your important documents so that they can be found later); a Personal Message Guide; and more.	The same documents are provided subject to the following limitations: • No legal consultation or specific drafting; • Short form documents rather than more comprehensive documents may be provided for Durable Power(s) of Attorney for Management of Property and Financial Affairs; and for Advance Health Care Directive(s). • Only one (1) California deed is included.

	Comprehensive Trust Package	Basic Trust Package (Do-It-Yourself package)
Consultation provided	The Comprehensive Trust Package includes up to 5 hours of legal consultation, explanation, and document review, and assistance with choosing the appropriate type of Trust, and assistance with funding your Trust, and detailed document drafting specific to your circumstances.	The Basic Trust Package includes no legal consultation nor time drafting specific language.
Presentation	Documents are printed on Hornstein security protection paper to help prevent tampering with your documents, and delivered to you in a comprehensive tabbed easy to follow binder.	The documents may be printed on plain paper.

PART 4 — GETTING AN AFFORDABLE AND APPROPRIATE ESTATE PLAN WITH HORNSTEIN LAW OFFICES THROUGH THE HORNSTEIN TRUST SYSTEM.

In this part of the Hornstein Trust Estate Planning Guide we will walk through all of the screens of the Hornstein Trust online questionnaire at www.HornsteinTrust.com. The questionnaire is among the most comprehensive estate planning questionnaires. Nevertheless, with helpful videos to guide you, it is among the easiest to navigate. You can use this part of the guide to help you on each screen of the questionnaire. You can also simply go to the online questionnaire itself. On each screen you can click to watch a video explaining the screen you are on, or you can click to read the explanation instead.

The following sections below provide information regarding each particular screen you will find on the HornsteinTrust.com website:

1. The Home Screen - Welcome to HornsteinTrust.com

From the Home Screen you will see when you first arrive at the HornsteinTrust.com website you can sign up for access to your free, no obligation, secure, personal Hornstein Trust questionnaire. Your questionnaire will help you to gather your thoughts on what you would like in your estate plan. If you have previously signed up, you can log in to your questionnaire from this Home screen.

The Home screen also provides information as follows:

Welcome to HornsteinTrust.com, the best place to get your living Trust, Will, Powers of Attorney, and all other necessary estate planning documents. Our mission is to help you plan and organize your financial affairs to protect you and your family. One of the most important actions you can take for your family is to obtain a complete and appropriate estate plan. We make getting a top quality estate plan easy and affordable.

Our informative videos will provide you guidance throughout and you can gather your thoughts in your personal, secure, no obligation Hornstein Trust questionnaire that you can easily complete at your convenience from your computer, iPad, or smartphone. At any time, you can call us for assistance or, if you are nearby, come in to our office to speak with one of our attorneys or paralegals.

If you don't need a Trust or you don't need anything, we'll know after reviewing your questionnaire with you. But, if you do need a Trust, there is no reason to put it off any longer. A Living Trust can avoid your family having to go to probate court to ask the Judge to allow your family access to your assets, and **save your family thousands to tens of thousands of dollars in probate fees and costs**. Let's consider Joe and Wendy who own a house in California, a car and a bank account but they have no estate plan. Since Joe and Wendy are the owner of their assets, they are the only ones who can sign a deed to their house. Only Joe and Wendy can handle other assets such as cars and money. **If Joe and Wendy die before they have put**

their house and other assets into a Trust, Joe and Wendy's family will have to go to court to ask the Judge to transfer their house, car, and bank account to them in a court proceeding called a **Probate**. If the house is worth $500,000, the probate will **cost more than $13,000** and likely **take a year or longer to complete**. And since the probate fees are based on the gross value of assets rather than the net value, if that $500,000 house has a $490,000 mortgage on it, the probate fees will be based on the $500,000, not the $10,000 of equity. **This wasted time and money going to court could have been avoided if Joe and Wendy simply had put their assets into a living Trust**.

Sign up now to access your **free, no obligation** Trust questionnaire, and we will send you, for **free** our **Hornstein Trust Estate Planning Guide – "Creating your Estate Plan – 18 Rules To Make Sure Your Estate Plan Will Work When It Needs To!"** This is your guide to estate planning and rules to follow to make sure your estate plan will work when it needs to. I'll give you **real life examples** of what can go wrong when the rules aren't followed, so that **you won't make these mistakes with your estate plan**.

A complete Hornstein Trust estate plan includes:

- **Living Trust**

- **Certificate of Trust**

- **Will(s)**

- **Durable Power(s) of Attorney**

- **Advance Health Care Directive(s)**

- **Physician's Directive(s)**

- **Funding Documents including a deed to your real property**

- **and more**

You can **learn more** about these important documents in our **Hornstein Trust Guide** or through our **informative videos you will find on your Trust questionnaire** or by **calling our office at (818) 887-9401 or (888) 280-8100** to speak with one of our attorneys or paralegals.

There are four easy steps to a top quality estate plan prepared by Hornstein Law Offices:

STEP 1: Enter your goals for your estate plan on your questionnaire.

STEP 2: Let our educational videos guide you through your questionnaire.

STEP 3: Print your questionnaire and review with us.

STEP 4: You decide when you are ready to hire us to draft your documents.

When you do choose to get your Trust through Hornstein Law Offices, you can rest assured it will be of the highest quality as we are a **multi-year winner of the Daily News Reader's Choice award for "Best Living Trust."** You may choose our award winning top quality "<u>Comprehensive Trust Package</u>" which **includes professional attorney consultation**. Or, if you have been looking for a Do-It-Yourself estate plan through the internet or Do-It-Yourself forms, then you can choose to do it yourself through our complete "**Basic Trust Package.**" Both packages are of the highest quality and value you will find anywhere. You can choose later which package you would like, or you can call us toll free for help in determining which one is right for you. Click on the <u>Information and Pricing</u> link for more information on the two packages.

The time to take action is now. There is no reason to keep your family at risk any longer. We look forward to including you in our family of clients. It costs you nothing to sign up to view your personal Hornstein Trust questionnaire. There is no charge until you hire us, and there is no obligation to hire us. If you need any assistance, please call us at (818) 887-9401 or toll free at **(888) 280-8100** to speak with one of our attorneys or paralegals. You can also email us at **support@ HornsteinTrust.com** and we will be happy to help you.

To access your personal Hornstein Trust questionnaire and receive for free our Hornstein Trust Guide and have access to our full series of videos, simply register as a new user by entering your name and email, and phone number. There is a simple math problem to solve so that we know you are not a robot. Next, simply click "Submit" and we will send you your **Free Hornstein Trust Guide** and you are on your way to accessing to your free no obligation personal Hornstein Trust questionnaire.

After clicking "Submit" you will be taken to the **Security Question and Password Screen** where you will have the option to add additional security to your questionnaire. Although you can choose to continue to your questionnaire without adding additional security, you are able to add a security question that you will need to answer in order to retrieve your current password (if you chose one) or choose a password (if you don't have one). If you don't choose an additional security question your default security question is your phone number that you entered on the Home Screen. You can also choose your password of six to ten characters from this screen. You don't have to choose your password yet but you will need a password in order to log in to your questionnaire after exiting your questionnaire. If you don't choose your password before exiting your questionnaire, from the Home Screen you can request to have a password generated for you and sent to your email. You will have to enter your phone number and also the answer to your security question if you chose one.

You have taken a big step towards protecting your family and your assets. We look forward to assisting you and hopefully, including you in our family of clients for whom we take pride in providing excellent service!

2. Client information

This is the first screen to begin to gather information to prepare your documents. Throughout this questionnaire you will see boxes along the right side of the screen. If you ever want to mark an area of the questionnaire for further follow up, just click on a box to the right of that section to put a check mark in it to remind yourself to follow up on that area of the questionnaire. Remember any time you have questions or comments on anything, just make note of it in the Notes box you will find at the bottom of every screen throughout your questionnaire.

First, you should indicate whether your Trust will be for one person or for two people by placing a check mark by "Single (one-person) Documents" or "Joint (two-person) Documents." Generally, a married couple will get a joint trust, which is one Trust that is for two people. A joint trust can hold the separate property of each spouse as well as the couple's community property. Generally speaking, separate property is property that a spouse acquired prior to getting married; but note that in order to prevent it from becoming community property, special care may be necessary to make sure it stays separate property. Community property is property that a married couple acquires during marriage. In certain circumstances, a married person could have a one-person trust for his or her separate property and a joint Trust with the spouse for the couple's community property.

If you are getting more than one Trust, such as if you and your spouse are getting separate Trusts to own each of your separate property, and a third separate Trust to own your community property, or if you would like to gather information to have a

Trust prepared for your parent(s) or adult child(ren), you will be able to create and access multiple questionnaires with a single login (email and password). Simply log out and log back in with your email and password to add additional questionnaires to store your information for each Trust. If you are anticipating getting multiple Trusts, and you would like assistance with such planning, please call us to discuss with one of our attorneys or paralegals. We will be happy to assist you and help you identify what you need to meet your goals for your estate plan.

After you indicate whether the Trust will be for one or two people, please enter your first name, your middle initial or middle name, and your last name as you would like them to appear in your documents. For your convenience, the entries are not case sensitive so you don't have to worry about whether to type in capital letters or small letters.

The questionnaire does not ask for your social security number. At the time of signing, you can write your social security number on your Certification of Trust to indicate the tax ID number that will be used for your Trust. Your Social Security number will be shown on your Certification of Trust, which a financial institution, such as a bank needs in order to open an account in the name of your Trust. The financial institution needs to know what tax ID number to put on account opening forms. If you are married, the tax ID number for the Trust can be the social security number of either spouse. The tax ID number for the portion of the Trust holding a spouse's separate property can be that particular spouse's social security number. You can have a separate Certification of Trust for the community property portion and for each spouse's separate property portion.

Next, enter your birthday, your address and your phone number, and indicate which phone number is the best number at which to reach you. When you enter your email address, note that this will not change the email address associated with your account when you initially signed up. If you would like to change the email address associated with your account, you may change this along with other account information in the "Account Settings" screen you will find at the upper left of each screen. If you need help adjusting your account settings, please call our office and we will be happy to help you. In fact, if you have questions on anything regarding your estate plan or your Trust questionnaire, just call us to help get you back on track.

Now you enter information regarding your marital status. Then enter whether you are a US citizen. Non-citizens will have particular estate tax planning issues that should be discussed with an attorney. Just mark it here and we'll review to see if there are issues that should be addressed.

Moving on, we have all of the same questions for the other person if you are getting a joint trust. Next, at the bottom of the screen is a box for you to make notes of any questions and comments you want to discuss with us. Finally, to save your answers, you must click the Save and Continue button. You will then be taken to the next screen. Remember that your information will not be saved unless you click the "Save and Continue" button to save your entries you just made on the current screen, or click any of the screens on the left, if you wish to visit screens in a different order.

3. Advisors

We often find it is helpful to involve your advisors in your estate planning process. Such advisors may include your lawyer, accountant, financial advisor, and your insurance agent. If you would like to allow us to contact your professional advisors to include them in the process of gathering relevant information that could help in creating appropriate documents for you, please list their name, email address and phone number on this screen. If helpful, we will contact them to let them know that you are working on an estate plan and that you have authorized us to speak with them to help gather information that may help us to prepare an appropriate estate plan to protect you and your family. Your advisors may likely require you to give them written permission to speak with us. If you would like your professional advisors to be able to make entries directly on your questionnaire, you may allow them to access your questionnaire by giving them your email and password to log in to your questionnaire. If you do release your username and password, I recommend that you only release these to your advisors who already have your sensitive information as well as an obligation to keep your information confidential through their professional relationship with you. Next, click the "Save and Continue" button at the bottom of the screen to save your answers.

4. Prior Marriages

If you or your spouse or domestic partner has had a prior marriage, please enter the name, how that marriage terminated, and the date of the termination of the marriage for each prior spouse. You can add a new prior marriage or delete any prior marriages entered by clicking the button to "Add Prior Marriage" or "Delete Prior Marriage." If you have no prior marriages, you may skip this screen and move on to the Living Children screen. We want to make sure that there are no issues with a prior spouse thinking they have an interest in your assets of your estate. If there are issues, we want to address them. Please write in the Notes box at the bottom of the screen any issues that you think may come up in the future. If there are no such issues and you really don't wish to mention any prior marriages in your document, then let us know that in the Notes box. Next, click the "Save and Continue" button at the bottom of the screen to save your answers.

5. Living Children

If you or your spouse or domestic partner have living children, please fill out this Living Children screen. Otherwise, skip this screen and move on to the Deceased Children screen. Please enter their name, birth date, whether they are male or female, and indicate the names of the parents. You can use the drop down menu to select a previously entered name to save you time from retyping information. Next, enter the address and phone numbers for each living child. You can add a child or delete a previously entered child by clicking on "Add Child" or "Delete Child" as necessary. If you don't have certain information with you now, just click on a "Flag for Follow up" box on the right side of the screen as a reminder to follow up on this. As always, if you have any questions or comments, just write that in the Notes box at the bottom of the screen. Next, click the "Save and Continue" button at the bottom of the screen to save your answers.

6. Deceased Children

If you or your spouse or domestic partner have deceased children, please fill out this Deceased Children screen. Otherwise skip this screen and move on to the Trustee and Executor screen. Please enter their name, birth date, whether they were male or female, and the names of the parents. As always, if you don't have certain information with you now, just click on a "Flag for Follow up" box on the right side of the screen as a reminder to follow up on this. If you have any questions or comments, just write that in the Notes box at the bottom of the screen. Next, click the "Save and Continue" button at the bottom of the screen to save your answers.

7. Trustee/Executor

Now is a good time to review the terms used to describe the

parties to, or the people involved in, a Trust. You are the owner of your assets, whether it is a bank account, real estate, or other property. And as the owner, you may be the manager of those assets as well in that you handle things. You write the checks on your bank account. You call your stock broker to buy and sell investments. You collect the rent from tenants on your rental property. And you are also the beneficiary of everything you own; your assets are to benefit you! People are used to being the owner, manager, and beneficiary of their own property whether it be bank accounts, real estate, or other property. However, when you have a Trust, these three parties are trifurcated into the Trustor, Trustee, and Beneficiary. The "Trustor," also referred to as "Settlor" or "Grantor" - any of these words ending in "or" - is the <u>Owner</u>. The "Trustee" also referred to as "Settlee" or "Grantee" - any of these words ending in "ee" – is the <u>Manager</u>. And finally, the <u>Beneficiary</u> is the one who is to benefit from the assets in the Trust.

When you set up a Trust, you will generally have yourself be all three during your life, or you and your spouse will be all three if you are married. You are the Trustor because you are the owner. You will generally also be the manager of your assets because you will make yourself the Trustee. Finally, you will likely also make yourself the beneficiary during your life because the one to benefit from your assets during your life is you! So you may be all three during your lifetime - the Trustor, the Trustee, and the Beneficiary, also known as the Owner, the Manager, and the one who is to benefit from the assets or enjoy the property.

You will always be the owner of property held by your Trust so you will always be the Trustor. Or, if you and your spouse or domestic partner are setting up the Trust together, then both of you may be the owners, or Trustors, of the Trust and of the property held by the Trust. However, you won't always be the Trustee of your Trust. When you pass away or if you become unable to act as Trustee, then another Trustee will take over that role of managing the Trust property. You can choose now who that other Trustee will be, in which case that other Trustee would be called the "Successor Trustee." In fact, you don't have to wait until you are incapacitated to have that other Trustee act. You could authorize another Trustee to act now, either alone or as a "co-Trustee" with you so that both of you can handle things. You can specify in your Trust whether one Trustee has authority to act alone or whether both Trustees have to act together. Typically, when there are co-Trustees, our Trusts provide that one Trustee can act alone in performing routine acts of administration, such as writing checks, but both Trustees must act together for major acts such as signing a deed to property.

We have had elderly clients who don't want to handle their own affairs anymore. Perhaps their son is helping them now anyway. If so, the Trust could simply make the son the Trustee now. Of course, the Client is still the Trustor (the Owner), and as Trustor, the Client, can amend (or change) his or her Trust to change who is the Trustee, either making himself or herself the Trustee or someone else the Trustee, and perhaps removing the son as a Trustee.

If you are going to be the current Trustee, which is typically the case, then you will choose a "Successor" Trustee to take over after you either pass away or are unable to handle your affairs. Generally, it is a good idea to choose a couple of alternates in case the Successor Trustee you choose predeceases you or is unable to handle it when the time comes. Who should be your successor Trustee? Often it may be one of your adult children. Or you can select your children and provide that they are to be Trustee only if they reach a certain age, such as age 18 or 21. Or you can select a sibling or friend to be your successor Trustee. It is often a good idea to choose someone who thinks the way you do, or if they don't, then you should provide more details in the Trust as to how the Trust should be managed. For example, suppose you provide in your Trust that funds be held for a child until the child reaches age 25, but until the child reaches age 25, the Trustee may make distributions to your child for their comfort and welfare, such as to buy a car when the child reaches age 16. If your successor Trustee thinks the way you do, you may not need to specify the type of car. But if your successor Trustee thinks a brand new top of the line BMW is an appropriate car for a 16 year old, then you may wish to include in your Trust that such car be a $5,000 car as adjusted for inflation. This would be addressed in the Beneficiary section of the Trust.

It is a good idea to choose someone that you trust and that thinks the way you do. You may not have someone like this in your life. In fact, you may have no one in your life that you trust. Or if you do have people in your life that you trust, they may not be responsible enough to handle the role of being trustee of your Trust. Or if you do have people in your life who you trust and are responsible, they may not be available to be trustee of your Trust. If you don't have anyone in your life who you trust and is responsible, and available to be trustee of your Trust, we can discuss having a professional trustee such as a bank or an independent professional fiduciary.

The term "fiduciary" is an important term. A Trustee has what is called a fiduciary duty. That means that they have an obligation to put the interests of the beneficiaries above their own. They must manage the Trust in the best interest of the beneficiaries.

Now, I'll discuss your <u>Will</u>. The term "Executor" refers to who will handle your Will. A Trustee handles the Trust. An Executor handles the Will. We generally have the Successor Trustees and your Executors be same people. After all, they are handling your property. A Trustee handles property owned by your Trust. An Executor handles property, after you pass away, that you didn't put into your Trust. Further, we will generally have your Agents under your Durable Power of Attorney for Management of Property and Financial Affairs, which is addressed later, also be these same people, because, again, the Trustee, and Executor, and Agent under a Financial Power of Attorney are all handling your property so it often makes sense to have these roles filled by the same people.

On this Trustee/Executor screen, check the box for "Yes" or "No" for the question, "Are the Settlor(s) to act as initial Trustee(s)?" The "initial Trustee" is the Trustee that you name to be the first Trustee of your Trust. Typically, you will act as the initial Trustee of your Trust. Thus, typically, you will answer this question with a "Yes" which means that you will be the initial Trustee, or the initial manager, of your Trust. If you select "No," then you would not be initial Trustee of your Trust, in which case, you would enter the name or names of who will be your initial Trustee or Trustees. If you select "Yes," then skip down to the "SUCCESSOR TRUSTEE(S)" section.

In the "SUCCESSOR TRUSTEE(S)" section, put the name of each person you would like to act as a Successor Trustee and put in order of who will be first, second, third, and so on. Typically, one may choose two Successor Trustees. But if one of your Successor Trustees is older than you are, then you may wish to add a third Successor Trustee in addition. When you pass away or cannot act as Trustee, then your first Successor Trustee will take over. If your first Successor Trustee is deceased or unable or unwilling to act, then your second Successor Trustee will take over, and so on. For each person you select to be a Trustee or Successor Trustee, enter their name, address, phone numbers, and their relationship to you – such as "Brother of Settlor," or if you and your spouse are the Settlors, then write whose brother he is.

Sometimes, a client may wish for two of their children to be co-Trustees. This may or may not be a good idea. I had a client whose father made her and her brother co-Trustees of the father's Trust. But they didn't think the same way. He moved fast and wanted everything done immediately. She moved slow and wanted to spend months looking through pictures and figuring out what to do. They couldn't work together, and got into arguments repeatedly. We had to go to court to reach a resolution. Before you make your children co-Trustees working together, consider issues that might arise or discuss this with us. Remember, it is often not a good idea to make someone Trustee so that they don't feel bad about not being named a Trustee. This is your Trust. You should have someone as Trustee who is going to follow your instructions and handle things the way you want them to be handled.

If you have any questions about who is an appropriate Trustee, or if you wish for Trustees to be co-Trustees, please write your thoughts in the Notes box at the bottom of the screen. As always, if you don't have certain information with you now, just click on a "Flag for Follow up" box to on the right side of the screen as a reminder to follow up on this. When you are ready to move on, click the "Save and Continue" button at the bottom of the screen to save your answers. Remember, you can always come back to this screen or any of the screens later.

8. Distribution of Remainder

On this screen, you will list the beneficiaries whom you wish to receive the remainder of your property after you pass away. By "remainder of your property," I mean what remains after any specific gifts you may designate. You will be asked to designate any specific gifts you wish to make on the next screen titled

"Gifts of Cash or Property."

When people have children, they often leave their assets or most of their assets to their children, but you don't have to do this. This is your Trust. You can leave your assets however you wish. For each beneficiary you name in your Trust, enter the percentage of the Trust assets that beneficiary should receive. Be sure the percentages for all beneficiaries total 100%.

After you choose beneficiaries, then select who the <u>alternate beneficiaries</u> will be. Most commonly, people choose the first option, which is "Issue by right of representation." This means that should a beneficiary pass away before you, that beneficiary's share will go to their "issue," which means to his or her children if they have children. And if a child predeceased you, then that child's share would go to that child's children, and so on. If a beneficiary has no issue, then the share would go to the surviving beneficiaries pro rata.

You may also select the second option, "Surviving beneficiaries," which means that should a beneficiary predecease you, that deceased beneficiary's share would NOT go to their issue (children, grandchildren, and so on), but instead will go to the surviving beneficiaries pro rata, that is, according to the relative percentages you provided in your Trust.

The third option is "Spouse of deceased beneficiary, but if such spouse predeceases Settlor(s), then issue of deceased beneficiary." The name of this option pretty much explains it.

For the fourth option, "Other," you can write the particular alternative beneficiary provision you desire. Please note that an additional fee may be required to review and draft particular language.

Next you will find on the "Distribution of Remainder" screen the section regarding "AGE/CONDITIONS FOR BENEFICIARY(IES) TO RECEIVE DISTRIBUTION." When you leave assets to a beneficiary through a Trust, you don't have to leave the assets outright. For example, you may not wish for your 12 year old child to inherit property outright. Also, a 12 year old would generally not be allowed by law to own such property outright. It would likely have to be held by a guardian for them until they turn 18, the age at which they are old enough to sign a contract. Most people also wouldn't want their 18-year old to inherit outright a large sum of money as it may encourage poor choices in life, such as not going to college or buying an inappropriate car.

This is one of the great benefits of having a Trust. You can specify ages at which you would like your children to inherit your assets. Many of my clients don't like to have their property go to their children until the children reach age 21 or 25. If you and your spouse place a high importance on education, you could provide that your property will be distributed outright to our children at the age 25 if they have graduated from a four-year accredited university. Otherwise, they have to wait until age 30. This option, or some variation of it, is popular because parents often have high educational aspirations for

STEVE H. HORNSTEIN, ESQ., CPA, LL.M., CFP®

their children, and they want to encourage them to reach those aspirations. Age 25 may make sense because that is usually two to three years after they will have graduated from college. They will have had two to three years to put their college degree to work for them before inheriting a sum of money. Also, by having to wait a few years after they graduate, instead of inheriting immediately upon graduation, they may be encouraged to not simply take easy courses to graduate in a hurry, but instead take courses that are meaningful to them and that they can use in a career. If you are not so particular that your child goes to a four year accredited university, you could simply require a "college degree" rather than a "degree from a four-year accredited university." The provisions you chose depend on your particular situation and what you desire for your children.

Through a Trust, you can choose a distribution that is appropriate to your family. For someone who is a college professor, and desires that her daughter place the same high importance on education as the parent, the parent can provide that her daughter receives 1/3 of the Trust estate upon her daughter receiving a bachelor's degree, then half of the balance upon her attaining a master's degree, and finally, the balance upon attaining a Ph.D.

It's your Trust, so in the box for "Distribution Age or Provision," select the distribution provision that makes sense for you.

- The first option is to distribute at a particular age. Age 21 is a popular choice as is age 25.

- The second option is to distribute the trust outright at a particular age, such as age 25, if the beneficiary has attained a particular educational goal, such as a "degree from a four-year accredited university," or a "college degree," which would include a two-year college degree. And if the educational goal has not been reached, then the beneficiary must wait until a later age, such as age 30. You can specify the ages that you would like, and you can specify which educational requirement you would like.

- The third option is to have half distributed at one age, such as age 25, and the balance at a later age, such as age 30.

- The fourth option is to split the distribution among three ages, such as one-third at age 25, half of the balance at age 30, and the balance at age 35.

If any of the beneficiaries mentioned are "Special Needs" beneficiaries, please note this in the area addressing this. A special needs beneficiary is a beneficiary who is receiving public benefits for a disability. For such beneficiaries, there are generally restrictions as to how much money or assets they can have, and if they have too much, they could lose their benefits. We can draft your trust to seek to protect the benefits for such beneficiaries. If you would like to discuss further, please check the "Flag for Follow Up " box and you can also write any particular questions in the Notes box at the bottom of the screen. Note that a Hornstein Trust includes a provision that should a beneficiary need a special needs trust to protect their benefits, a special needs trust will be set up for that purpose as allowed by law. When you are ready to move on, click the "Save and Continue" button at the bottom of the screen to save your answers and move on to the next screen.

9. Specific Gifts of Cash or Property

On the Specific Gifts of Cash or Property screen, you list particular gifts of cash or property you would like to make to beneficiaries upon the death of the Settlor, or both Settlors if you and your spouse or domestic partner are the Settlors. The distribution of the remainder of the Trust will be addressed on the next screen. When it comes time to distribute the Trust, the specific gifts are distributed first, and then the remainder is distributed according to your instructions provided in your Trust. To provide examples of specific gifts, you may wish to make a gift of $1,000 to a friend and $2,000 to a charity such as The Red Cross. These gifts are specific gifts that should be addressed on this screen. If you leave a gift to a charity, please be clear as to which charity is to receive the gift. There has been litigation between charities over gifts when the particulars are not mentioned. For example, if you leave money to a charity such as the Red Cross, investigate whether you need to name a particular branch or division or geographic area so that two divisions are not fighting over the money later. Perhaps we will have to write it as The Red Cross of Los Angeles to indicate the specific city branch and it is a good idea to also write the phone number and address to make it clear who is the correct beneficiary. If you want particular gifts to be made upon the passing of one spouse or domestic partner, or a particular spouse or domestic partner, you can note that in the box for the "Amount or Description of Gift". For example, if you want the piano to be distributed to someone upon the passing of the husband only rather than upon the passing of both husband and wife, indicate this in that box.

One spouse can provide that his or her motorcycle is to be distributed to one child upon the passing of that spouse, while the other spouse can provide that his or her jewelry or watch collection or a specific watch goes to another child upon that spouse's passing. Also, if you want to wait until the beneficiary reaches a certain age , please note this as well in the "Amount or Description of Gift" box.

If you are leaving a large specific gift, you may wish to limit it to a maximum percentage of the Trust so that the gift does not consume too large a portion of the Trust. For example, if you make a gift of $100,000 to a friend, and you currently have a net worth of $1 million, consider having the gift be written in the "Amount or Description of Gift" box as "$100,000 not to exceed 10% of the Trust." This way, if your estate is only worth $200,000 upon your passing, this gift of $100,000 will be reduced to a $20,000 gift (10% of $200,000), so that it does not consume a greater portion of your Total trust than you intend.

If you wish to add a beneficiary, simply click on "Add a Beneficiary" and to delete a beneficiary, simply click on

"Delete a Beneficiary." If you have any questions or issues you would like to discuss, please write these questions and issues in the Notes box at the bottom of the screen. Finally, when you are ready to move on, click the "Save and Continue" button at the bottom of the screen to save your answers and move on to the "Guardian(s) of Minor(s) screen.

10. Guardian(s) of Minor(s)

On the Guardian(s) of Minor(s) screen, you or you and your spouse or domestic partner will list who you wish to be guardians for your minor children. This will be specified in your Will rather than your Trust, as the Trust governs property, and children are not "property." If you and your spouse or domestic partner have children together, then each of your provisions for guardians should be the same to avoid conflicting provisions in each of your Wills. I recommend you discuss this together to determine who you both feel will raise your kids in a manner that matches how you would like them to be raised. Consider factors such as where you wish your children to live, religion, and how the guardian emphasizes education, and parenting style. Also, you may wish to consider the age of the guardians you list. If your first choice for a guardian is much older than you, you may wish to choose a successor guardian who is younger in case your first choice is unable to do it. Note that you do not have to have your Successor Trustee be your chosen guardian also. Your successor Trustee handles money and property owned by the Trust. Your chosen guardian will handle the raising of your children. Choose the persons you feel will be most appropriate for each role.

As you complete this screen, if you would like to discuss anything further, please check the "Flag for Follow Up " box and you can also write any particular questions in the Notes box at the bottom of the screen. When you are ready to move on, click the "Save and Continue" button at the bottom of the screen to save your answers and move on to the next screen.

11. Durable Power of Attorney for Management of Property

On the Durable Power of Attorney for Management of Property screen, you will provide who you wish to handle your financial affairs if you become unable to handle them. For example, for an older person, this issue could arise when an elderly person has dementia. Or for a younger person, if someone is in a car accident and in the hospital for a few weeks, who will handle paying your bills? If you are in the hospital longer, who will handle the various other financial matters that may be needed? Now, typically, your successor Trustee will take over issues dealing with the Trust until you are able to resume your duties, but there may be matters which the Trust does not cover. If you have a bank account that you did not put into the Trust, or perhaps if someone needs to contact and speak with your insurance company or file your tax return, there may be no one authorized to handle these issues unless you authorize someone to handle them. In the Durable Power of Attorney (or DPA) for Management of Property, you will authorize someone to handle these issues. The parties to a DPA are the "Agent" and the "Principal." The person you authorize to stand in your shoes to act on your behalf is called your "Agent." You are the "Principal" since you are the one authorizing someone, your agent, to act on your behalf. An Agent acting on behalf of the Principal under a DPA has a legal obligation called a "fiduciary duty" to act in the best interest of the principal.

Generally, since an agent under your DPA for management of property handles money and property, you will generally have the same person who you chose to be your Successor Trustee of your Trust and Executor of your Will to also be your agent under your DPA. If you don't, it could potentially cause some overlap or confusion in some of the work your agent and Successor Trustee are doing on your behalf. If you are married or have a domestic partner, you will generally choose your spouse or domestic partner to be your first agent, and then for your successor agents, you will generally choose the same people, and in the same order, that you chose to be the Successor Trustees of your Trust. If you want your agents to be different from your Trustees, you can, but perhaps we can discuss your reasons for this so that we understand the issues.

On this screen, please enter the people you would like to have as your agents on your Durable Power of Attorney for Management of Property. For your convenience, you can select a person you previously entered, or you can retype the information. As always, as you complete this screen, if you would like to discuss anything further, please check the "Flag for Follow Up" box and you can also write any particular questions in the Notes box at the bottom of the screen. When you are ready to move on, click the "Save and Continue" button at the bottom of the screen to save your answers and move on to the next screen.

12. Advance Health Care Directive

The Advance Health Care Directive / Durable Power of Attorney for Health Care screen has several sections. At the top of this screen, you, or you and your spouse or domestic partner, will select who you wish to make health care decisions for you in case you are unable to do so. Such decisions may include which hospital you should be at, or which doctor you should see, or whether a certain medical procedure should be done or not. The document in which you specify who will make health care decisions for you is called an Advance Health Care Directive or a Durable Power of Attorney (or "DPA") for Health Care. As with the DPA for Management of Property, the person you choose is called your "Agent" and you are the "Principal." You do not have to choose the same people you chose to be your agents under your DPA for Management of Property to also be your agents under your DPA for Health Care. It is common for someone to choose someone who is good with financial matters to be their Successor Trustee for their Trust, Executor for their Will, and their Agent for their DPA for Management of Property, while they choose someone else who is good with health care matters to be their agent under their DPA for Health Care. If you are married or you have a domestic partner, generally, you may wish to have your spouse or domestic partner be your first agent under your DPA for Health Care. For you and your spouse or domestic partner, each of you may choose different people to be your agents and your successor agents to make health care decisions for each of you.

On this screen, please enter who you wish to be your agents under your Durable Power of Attorney for Health Care. For your convenience, you can select a person you previously entered, or you can retype the information. As always, as you complete this screen, if you would like to discuss anything further, please check the "Flag for Follow Up " box and you can also write any particular questions in the Notes box at the bottom of this section of screen.

The next section of this screen is the Advance Medical Directive or Physician's Medical Directive. Most people generally do NOT wish to leave to their agent in their DPA for Health Care the responsibility of making decisions regarding whether to use life prolonging measures. Such a decision is often a very difficult and emotional decision for someone to make on behalf of another person. You can make this decision now in your Physician's Directive so that you do not have to burden anyone else with this decision. Please select the sentence that best describes what you would like for yourself regarding life sustaining procedures. Your choices are as follows:

a) I do not wish to receive medical treatment if I am in

an irreversible coma or persistent vegetative state; or terminally ill and life-sustaining procedures would only artificially delay death; or otherwise if burdens of treatment outweighs expected benefits.

b) I want to receive medical treatment that will allow me to live as long as possible.

If you have a spouse or domestic partner, each of you may make different choices. While I find that approximately 99% choose option (a), there is no right or wrong answer. The importance of making this decision for yourself made headlines with the legal battle involving Terri Schiavo in which Terri's husband and Terri's parents fought a very public battle in the Florida courts for seven years from 1998 until 2005 over the issue of whether to discontinue life prolonging measures. On February 25, 1990, Terri Shiavo suffered brain damage due to a lack of oxygen after collapsing in her home in full cardiac arrest. After two and a half months in a coma, her doctors changed her diagnosis to "vegetative state," and for the next two years her doctors tried therapy, without success, to increase her awareness. Finally, in 1998 Terri's husband filed a petition in court to have her feeding tube removed. Terri's parents opposed the petition. At one point her feeding tube was removed, only to be reinserted a few days later. Finally, after fourteen appeals and numerous other motions, petitions, and hearings, her feeding tube was finally removed for the last time on March 18, 2005, and she died thirteen days later. She had been in a coma for over fifteen years.

The case has been discussed and debated for years on issues including the sanctity of life, religion, and public policy. Both Terri Schiavo's husband and parents have written books on the case. While differing viewpoints remain among people, the legal battle started because of differing viewpoints of Terri Schiavo's husband and her parents. Determining which side was or is right or wrong from a public policy standpoint is not what a Physician's Directive seeks to answer. The purpose of the Physician's Directive is to inform your doctor what you think is right for YOU. "What would Terri Schavio have wanted for herself?" It was most unfortunate that Terri Schiavo's family never had a clear answer to this question because she never signed a physician's directive. It is a very important decision of whether to prolong your life by extraordinary measures when you are terminally ill or in a persistent vegetative state. Some may view it as cruel to leave the responsibility for making this decision on your behalf to someone else. Can you see yourself leaving to your children or parents this decision of whether or not to keep you alive? If you don't have a Physician's Directive, then you are leaving this decision to someone else. The Physician's Directive is the document in which you make the decision for yourself as to what you want for yourself as it pertains to using extraordinary measures to keep you alive when you are terminally ill or in a persistent vegetative state.

The next section of this screen asks three questions addressing your wishes regarding anatomical bequests, plans regarding the disposition of your remains, such as burial or cremation, and authorization of autopsy. At the first question, please select yes or no as to whether you would like your agent to allow anatomical bequests. I remember when the first heart transplant patient lived approximately a week. Today, I know two people who have received heart transplants, including an individual who has survived more than ten years after receiving a heart from a donor, and this individual is in his 70's. These days, transplant patients receive corneas allowing them to see, or kidneys or other organs allowing them to live productive lives with their families and friends. While it is a wonderful thing to provide someone else the opportunity to live or live a better life, this is a personal decision. It is for you to make the decision that is best for you, considering your family, your religious beliefs, and how you feel. Always remember that there is no right or wrong answer. There is just the answer that is best for you. These are your documents.

Next, if you have any plans regarding the disposition of your remains, such as burial or cremation, you can write that in the box provided. You can write the name and address and phone number of the mortuary, and indicate what you have prepaid. Or, you can simply write "Leave to Agent's discretion," or you can write simply "Cremation" or "Burial" or you can provide for burial at a cemetery of your particular religion or location. Whatever you don't specify will be left to your agent's discretion.

Next, please answer yes or no as to whether you would like your agent to authorize an autopsy. An autopsy is generally not always performed, but may be desired in cases of crime or public safety, that is, to solve a crime or resolve a public safety concern, such as discovering or tracking a new strain of flu. However, if you have strong beliefs about not having an autopsy, you can indicate that here by checking "No."

As always, as you complete this screen, if you don't know an answer now or you would like to discuss or simply follow up with a question later, please check the "Flag for Follow Up" box, and you can also write any particular questions in the Notes box at the bottom of the screen. When you are ready to move on, click the "Save and Continue" button at the bottom of the screen to save your answers and move on to the next screen.

13. Asset Ledger

The Asset Ledger Screen is important in order to determine what should be **funded** into your Trust and to determine assets for which you need to confirm or change the beneficiary. As Rule #8 of the Hornstein Trust Guide explains, an expensive probate may be required if you don't have a trust ***and also properly fund your assets into your Trust***. And this may be the reason you are going to the Hornstein Trust site – to avoid a probate! Therefore, funding your Trust is extremely important. One asset that will typically be funded into your Trust will be any real estate that you own, such as your house. We can prepare these deeds and help you to record the deeds with the county recorder. Your other assets should be reviewed as well to make sure they are properly handled. When your Hornstein Trust book is completed, you will receive instructions to help you in funding your Trust, but if you need more assistance, just let us know and we can help you to make sure that the funding of your trust is handled properly. The funding of your Trust starts with the information you enter on this screen.

On this screen we want to identify your assets that will need to be funded into your Trust, and we want to identify the assets that should NOT be funded into your Trust. While it is important to actually fund your Trust with assets that should be in your Trust, it is just as important to NOT fund into your Trust assets that should NOT be in your Trust. The type of asset will determine how it is treated. Whether the type of asset is a "Qualified" or "Non-qualified" asset will determine whether you should fund the asset into your Trust or whether instead you should have a beneficiary form on file with the financial institution. When you enter your assets on this screen, we will be able to prepare the proper funding documents and inform you how each asset should be treated.

Please enter information on your assets on this screen. As you complete this screen, if you don't know an answer now or you would like to discuss with us or simply follow up later, please check the "Flag for Follow Up " box and you can also write any particular questions or concerns in the Notes box at the bottom of the screen. When you are ready to move on, click the "Save and Continue" button at the bottom of the screen to save your answers and move on to the next screen. And always know that you can follow up with a phone call or an email or a personal visit to my office with questions or assistance in making sure that your Trust is properly funded.

14. Additional Notes and Questions

Having now reached the Additional Notes and Questions screen, I say "Congratulations, you are almost at the end of your questionnaire." You have entered a lot of information and hopefully learned a lot about estate planning from the videos throughout the questionnaire and the Hornstein Trust Estate Planning Guide. And quite likely, going through this questionnaire has caused you to think about issues and questions you haven't thought about before. This is a good thing. You should be thinking about these various issues involving your family and friends, because it will help you to develop your ideas as to how you would like your estate plan to be drafted. If some issues and questions are at the forefront of your mind now, write them down now in the Notes box on this screen before you forget. If anything comes to mind later, just log back in with your e-mail and password, click on the "Additional Notes and Questions" link and type in your thoughts. We can review your thoughts with you and determine how to incorporate them into your documents. Such questions may be, "Should I make a separate provision for my dog or cat?" If that is your question, we can discuss your simply having your pet go to your designated beneficiary, or we can discuss adding a "pet trust" to your documents. You may have a question as to whether it is a good idea to have one of your children be your first successor trustee, and another child be your second successor trustee, or whether you should have two of your children be co-trustees acting together. If that is your question, we can discuss one of the court cases I had that is mentioned at Rule #7 of the Hornstein Trust Guide. In one of these cases, a father made his son and daughter co-trustees, maybe hoping that this would be a good opportunity for his kids to finally work together after never having worked together before. In this case, it wasn't a good idea. They had different ways of doing things. His son liked to move fast and wanted to sell the house right away, and his daughter liked to move at a slower pace. They couldn't work together. Had I been able to speak with that father prior to him signing his Trust, I would have discussed with him the characteristics of his children, and which one managed their affairs the way the father would like his Trust to be managed. For any issue and questions that come to mind, simply jot them down on this screen. Such issues may be things you want to discuss with my office, or questions you want to discuss with your family or with your other advisors, or simply issues and questions you want to think about further. The point is, jot them down, so you don't forget about them.

I also provide information as to how we will name your Trust. If you wish to have a particular name for your Trust, you can indicate this in the Notes at the bottom of the screen. Next, please inform us if you already have a Trust and this Trust will be amending and restating that existing Trust. Of course, please call our office or email us at Support@HornsteinTrust.com if you have any questions. When you are ready to move on, click the "Save and Continue" button at the bottom of the screen to save your answers and move on to the next screen.

15. Disclosure and Compliance

The Disclosure and Compliance screen has important disclosures and compliance information of which you should be aware. For example, you should understand the difference in working with a paralegal and an attorney, and you should understand that you are ultimately responsible for funding your Trust. You should understand that we recommend that you consult with your tax advisor for tax advice. And while it is common for us to represent both a husband and a wife together in the preparation of a Trust, I need to make you aware of the possibility that a conflict of interest could arise, and what happens if it does. Please read this screen and when you have finished, please click the "save and continue" button to continue to the next screen.

16. Service Agreement

The Service Agreement screen describes the two types of trust packages as well as other services we offer. Please read about the differences between the *Comprehensive Trust Package* and the *Basic Trust Package*. Note that our typical client chooses the Comprehensive Trust Package, as this package allows us to provide greater assistance to make sure the Trust is completed, signed, and funded properly. Nevertheless, we recognize that there are "do-it-yourselfers" who wish to do things on their own, and who might otherwise not get a Trust at all if they had to pay more than a "Do-It-Yourself" Trust cost. For these clients, we offer The Basic Trust Package. While you will likely find the Hornstein Trust Basic Trust Package is more comprehensive and of higher quality than "Do It Yourself" trust packages offered by many other companies either in stores or on the internet, we still suggest that the Basic Trust Package be selected only by sophisticated individuals who have taken the time to educate themselves in the estate planning process and are willing to take on some additional risks in regards to assuring their estate plans are complete, accurate and funded properly. Reading the Hornstein Trust Estate Planning Guide, "**18 Rules To Make Sure Your Estate Plan Will Work When It Needs To!**" is a great place to start in your estate planning process.

Please read below and choose which package you would like. If you are unsure at this time, you can call our office and speak with us and we will help you to decide. If you have a question that hasn't been answered through this site, just jot it down and ask us. Also shown are some à la carte services, such as if you only want a deed or a durable power of attorney and don't want a complete Trust package. Again, discuss with us if you have any questions.

Please note that the fee charged by the notary to notarize your signatures and the fee charged by a County Recorder's office to record your deed to your property are not included and will need to be paid separately to the notary or the county recorder. We can help you locate a notary, and assist you in having your deeds recorded with the appropriate County Recorder. In California, we can often arrange for a notary to come to see you, but they may charge extra to travel. You can also come to our office if you are nearby and we can arrange for a notary to notarize your documents at our office. Typically, the notary fees are in the range of $90 to $105 for a single person Trust Book, and $180 to $210 for a joint or married couple Trust Book. It could be more if you need assignments of interest of businesses or if you have multiple properties requiring deeds. If the cost of a notary is difficult for you, you may wish to check with your bank as some banks in which you have a large account may offer to notarize your documents free of charge. However, because there are so many documents, the notary at the bank may not be willing to notarize all of the documents for free. Also, it is often helpful to have a notary who is experienced with notarizing estate planning documents, but it may not be necessary if you are very careful during the signing process not to miss anything.

There is one item that I suggest you add to your Trust Package, and that is having your documents scanned onto a CD or flash drive after they are signed. The additional cost is $250 but I think it is well worth it. Here's why. Discussed at Rule #2 of the Hornstein Trust Guide, my first case that went all the way to trial involved someone who passed away and the family could not find his Trust. It was lost. We had an unsigned copy from the computer files from the law firm who drafted it, but we did not have the original. The copy showed that the beneficiaries were one-half to his girlfriend of twenty years and one half to his son from his estranged wife from whom he had legally separated thirty years earlier but never finalized the divorce. Yes, I know what you might be thinking – yet another example of someone procrastinating and not following through to make sure his affairs are in order. Sound familiar? Well, in this case we represented the girlfriend. If we could prove the Trust existed as the copy showed, the girlfriend and the son would get it. If we couldn't, the Probate Code provided that property would go one-half to the wife and one-half to the son. The son would get half anyway, so it was a battle between the girlfriend of 20 years and the estranged wife of 30 years. I presented the copy of the Trust to the wise Judge and the Judge asked me, "How do I know that that is the Trust he signed?" I answered, "Well, in the ordinary course of business, the attorney who drafted the Trust saved the files in his computer and this is the last version of the Trust in his computer." The judge asked again, "OK, but how do I know that THIS copy in my hand is a copy of the one that he signed?" I answered again, "In the ordinary course of business, the attorney who drafted the Trust saved the files in his computer and this is the last version of the Trust in his computer." The Judge and I went back and forth with this a few times, until I realized the issue and said, "You're right, your honor. We don't know." Because really, the attorney could have made changes to the Trust in his computer, printed it for signing, and then closed the computer file without saving it, in which case the Trust that he signed would not match the file in the computer. So, we had a four day trial in which we did ultimately prove by testimony of friends and family that it was the girlfriend and NOT the wife who was the beneficiary, and then the wife appealed and we went to appeals, and the appellate court upheld the Judge in the trial court. We eventually won, but it took years. If we only had a ***signed*** copy of the Trust, I could have held that up to the Judge and said, "You honor, we know this is the Trust he signed because this is a ***signed*** copy and his signature is right here!" We would likely have been done in one day. It was because of this case that we made available to our clients having us scan a signed copy of the complete Trust Book so that if any of the documents in your Trust Book are ever lost, either because it was misplaced or destroyed in a flood or a fire, we could always print another copy of the "signed" document from our scanned file. And, your family also could have it to store on a computer or on CD or flashdrive. The cost is $250 and it is entirely optional - but I recommend it.

You are almost done. Up to this point, you may still have not hired us to do anything for you, and you are under no obligation to hire us. But if you do hire us, you'll be happy that you did, because our Trust Book is of the highest quality and value you will find anywhere. If you would like to hire us to help you, simply fill out the information at the bottom of the screen. Typically, from the time we have all required information, we can complete your Trust Book in one to three weeks. However, if there is any particular date by which you need it finished, such as for example, if you are going on a vacation soon and you really want it done by then, please enter that date where indicated below. If our staff has to work overtime to get it done, we may need to charge extra for the rush, but we'll let you know if this is the case. We can often simply adjust our work schedule to get it done when you want it. In the Minimum Fee section, enter the number when adding up the costs you selected above. If you would like to pay less than the minimum fee up front, you can call our office for the required amount of deposit. Otherwise, you can simply leave the Deposit field blank. Then fill out the rest with your name and payment information. Please note that we still must accept you as a client. If there are any problems, such as if it appears from your questionnaire that you have particular needs that my firm cannot fulfill, or if there is a conflict, we will let you know. As always, if you have any questions, just call us or send an e-mail to Support@HornsteinTrust.com. When you are ready to move on, even if you haven't yet decided to hire us to help you, click the "Save and Continue" button at the bottom of the screen to save your entries and move on to the next screen, where you will have the opportunity to print your complete questionnaire as you have it thus far.

17. Wrap up and Review

You have arrived at the Wrap up and Review screen. If you are on this screen, then "Congratulations!" You have finished your questionnaire. You have just taken a very big step towards having your complete estate plan prepared. The next step will be a discussion with an attorney or paralegal at my office to make sure that all of your issues and questions have been addressed. The discussion may be brief or lengthy depending on your issues and questions, and what you would like us to do for you. Then when you are ready, we'll complete the documents you have hired us to complete, and when they are completed, we'll deliver them to you, along with detailed instructions to explain how to sign and fund your Trust.

On this screen, you can choose to print your complete questionnaire or various sections of your questionnaire as you have it thus far. Just select what you would like to print and click on the "Print Questionnaire" button. If you haven't already hired us to prepare your documents, we hope that you have selected or will select us to assist you with this very important step in your life to protect you and your family with a complete Trust and estate plan, and we look forward to working with you. When you are ready to log out, click the "Log Out" button. You can log back in to your questionnaire with your email and password at www.HornsteinTrust.com any time that is convenient for you 24/7, from your computer, smartphone, or tablet.

IN CLOSING

In closing, I want to thank you and congratulate you for taking the time to read my book and start your estate plan. Please call my office if we can be of any help to you and your family.

Made in the USA
Lexington, KY
13 December 2019